More Sweet Treats

More Sweet Treats

Recipes from the Moonglow Christmas Series

Deborah Garner

Cranberry Cove Press

Copyright © 2024 Deborah Garner

Cranberry Cove Press / Published by arrangement with the author

More Sweet Treats by Deborah Garner

All rights reserved. Except for brief text quoted and appropriately cited in other works, no part of this book may be reproduced in any form, by photocopying or by electronic or mechanical means, including information-storage-or-retrieval systems, without permission in writing from the copyright owner/author.

Cranberry Cove Press, PO Box 1671, Jackson, WY 83001, United States

Cover design by Mariah Sinclair | www.mariahsinclair.com

Library of Congress Catalog-in-Publication Data Available

Garner, Deborah

More Sweet Treats/ Deborah Garner—1st United States edition 1. Fiction 2. Woman Authors 3. Holidays

p. cm.

978-1-952140-32-7 (paperback)

Printed in the United States of America

10 9 8 7 6 5 4 3 2

Books by Deborah Garner

The Paige MacKenzie Mystery Series
Above the Bridge
The Moonglow Café
Three Silver Doves
Hutchins Creek Cache
Crazy Fox Ranch
Sweet Sierra Gulch

The Moonglow Christmas Novella Series
Mistletoe at Moonglow
Silver Bells at Moonglow
Gingerbread at Moonglow
Nutcracker Sweets at Moonglow
Snowfall at Moonglow
Yuletide at Moonglow
Starlight at Moonglow
Joy at Moonglow
Evergreen Wishes at Moonglow
Angels at Moongloow

The Sadie Kramer Flair Series
A Flair for Chardonnay
A Flair for Drama
A Flair for Beignets
A Flair for Truffles
A Flair for Flip-Flops

A Flair for Goblins
A Flair for Shamrocks

Cranberry Bluff
Sweet Treats
More Sweet Treats

To the amazing readers of the Moonglow Christmas Series who share recipes for others to enjoy, and to all those who enjoy sweet treats.

Contents

RECIPES FROM YULETIDE AT MOONGLOW	1
Glazed Cinnamon Nuts—A Family Recipe	3
Yuletide Coconut Cherry Cookies	4
Candy Bar Pretzel Cookies	6
Chocolate Almond Coconut Cookies	8
Mary's Sugar Cookies	9
Chocolate Crinkle Cookies	10
Applesauce Cookies	12
Chocolate-Dipped Shortbread	13
Ethyl's Chocolate Fudge	15
Sugar Cakes	16
Buttercream Candy	17
Black Walnut Cookies	18
Sunflower Refrigerator Cookies	19
Pretzel Chocolate Bites	20
Ethyl's Oatmeal Raisin Cookies	21
Goldbricks	22
Lemon Blueberry Scones	23
Chocolate Sandwich Cheesecake Cookies	25
Peanut Butter Muffins	27
Snowballs	28
Rudolph's Oatmeal Cookies	29
RECIPES FROM STARLIGHT AT MOONGLOW	31
Santa's Favorite Chocolate Cookies	33
Eggnog Cookie with Rum Butter Icing	35
Apple Pie Cookies	37
Cherry Scones	38
Aunt Nellie's PB Surprise	40
Christmas Snow Clouds	41
Whipped Chocolate Chip Shortbread Cookies	42
Sugar-Free Orange Cookies	43

Cranberry White Chocolate Bars	44
Rhubarb Cookies	45
Cherry Brownie Bon Bons	46
Impossible Peanut Butter Cookies	48
Caramel Popcorn Balls	49
Mom's Angel Pie	50
Amish Sugar Cookies	51
Grinch Cookies	52
Chai Tea Shortbread Cookies	54
Nutella Hazelnut Brownies	56
Peanut Butter Chocolate Fudge	57
Christmas Dreams	58
RECIPES FROM JOY AT MOONGLOW	59
Christmas Hugs and Kisses Cookies	61
Peppermint Snowball Cookies	63
Peanut Butter Cocoa Drops	65
Gluten-Free Apple Cookies	66
No-Bake Gluten-Free Cookies	67
Raspberry Bars	68
Coconut Oatmeal Cookies	69
Hearty Banana Tea Loaves/Muffins	70
Double-Chocolate Lemon Cookies	71
Mocha Peppermint Cookies	73
Cranberry Almond Scone Cookies	74
Mexican Wedding Cakes	75
Banana Oatmeal Cookies	76
Lila's Lace Cookies	78
Holly Cookies	79
Chocolate Waffle Cookies	80
Chocolate Crinkle Cookies	81
Easy Peanut Butter Cookies	83
Chocolate-Dipped Shortbread Cookies	84
Cranberry Orange Cookies	86
Raspberry Almond Cookies	88
Cranberry Walnut Pinwheel Cookies	89
Mini Cranberry Tarts	91

RECIPES FROM EVERGREEN WISHES AT MOONGLOW	92
Chocolate-Dipped Orange Butter Cookies	94
Sugar Cookies	95
Christmas Popcorn	96
Chocolate Candy Cane Fudge	97
Ice Box Fruitcake	98
Dayna's Oatmeal Cookies	99
Date Nut Torte Squares	100
Salted Peanut Cookies	101
Cranberry White Chocolate Bars	102
Caramel Apple Cookies	103
Gluten-Free Chocolate Chip Cookies	105
Pecan Cheese Wafers	106
Gingerbread Kiss Cookies	107
Million-Dollar Fudge	109
Almond Crunch Bars	110
Pecan Fingers	111
Momma's Sour Cream Walnuts	112
Red Velvet Cake Cookies	113
Cheesecake Stuffed Strawberry Cookies	115
Graham Cracker Toffee Bars	117
Wassail	119
RECIPES FROM ANGELS AT MOONGLOW	120
Snowball Cookies	122
Frosted Gingerbread Cookies	123
Josie's Fudge	125
Crème Brûlée Cookies	126
Easy Christmas Bark	128
Orange Crisps	129
Gingerbread Sandwich Cookies	130
The Best Old-Fashioned Molasses Sugar Cookies	132
Crackle Double Chocolate Cookies	134
Walnut Butter Cookies	135
Glazed Fruitcake Cookies	136

Dutch Letter Almond Bars	138
Red Velvet Cupcakes	139
Sour Cream Sugar Cookies	142
Rolo Cookie Bars (Gluten-Free Version)	143
Sparkling Angel Cookies	145
Pecan Kisses	147
Old-Fashioned Sugar Cookies	148
Iced Peppermint Candy Cookies	149
Recipe Notes	151
Recipe Notes	153
Books by Deborah Garner	155
About the Author	165

Recipes from Yuletide at Moonglow

Deborah Garner

Excerpt from *Yuletide at Moonglow*

Mist stood in the kitchen door, one slender hand lightly touching the doorframe, and watched the activity in the café. It warmed her heart to see Betty entertain other locals, to hear the cheerful chatter, to listen to shared stories about family recipes as each participant contributed a batch of something delicious. The annual cookie exchange was Betty's pride and joy, a yearly activity she'd held long before Mist came to Timberton.

"I can only stay a few minutes," Marge said as she swooped in with a cellophane-covered plate. Her hair was clipped up away from her face, and she wore a work apron with a candy cane print. "The shop is busy today. Thank heavens I have two extra workers to help with candy sales during the holidays. I just had to get these buttercream candies over here to share."

Betty took the cookies with one hand and gave Marge a one-armed hug. A blinking nose from a reindeer on Betty's sweatshirt flashed a red light against the cellophane covering the plate. "So happy you could make it. These look delicious!"

Marge was soon joined by Millie, who held a tray of chocolate crinkle cookies. Clayton's mother followed with a tray of coconut almond treats. The enthusiastic arrival of participants continued, and selections on the tables grew. Gingerbread men and women, chocolate fudge, and baked confections of all sorts soon filled the room, and assortments came together for each person to take home.

"I love this event," Betty said, taking a break to stop by the kitchen door and visit with Mist.

"And they love it just as much," Mist said. "That's one of the lovely things about tradition. We get to look forward to the event, and we get to look back fondly on the memories."

Glazed Cinnamon Nuts – A Family Recipe

Ingredients:

1 cup sugar
¼ cup water
⅛ teaspoon cream of tartar
Heaping teaspoon of cinnamon
1 tablespoon butter
1 ½ cups walnut halves

Directions:

Boil sugar, water, cream of tartar and cinnamon to soft ball stage (236 degrees).
Remove from heat.
Add butter and walnuts.
Stir until walnuts separate.
Place on wax paper to cool.

Yuletide Coconut Cherry Cookies

(Submitted by Kim Davis)

Snowy-white coconut and glistening red cherries add holiday cheer to these shortbread-style cookies, making them an ideal addition to Christmas cookie platters. Makes 18–20 cookies.

Ingredients:

½ cup room temperature unsalted butter (substitute vegan margarine if desired, to make suitable for vegans)
½ cup granulated sugar
¼ teaspoon almond extract
1-⅓ cups all-purpose flour
1 teaspoon baking powder
½ teaspoon salt (if using margarine, omit)
1 cup sweetened coconut flakes
20 small maraschino cherries, divided

Directions:

Drain the maraschino cherries. Cut 10 of the cherries in half, pat dry and set aside. Coarsely chop the remaining cherries, blot excess liquid, and set aside.

Cream together the butter (or margarine), sugar, and almond extract, for 2 minutes.

Whisk together the flour, baking powder, and salt, then stir into the butter mixture until incorporated.

Gently fold the reserved coarsely chopped cherries into the cookie dough.

Cover dough with plastic wrap and refrigerate 1 hour.

Preheat oven to 350 degrees.

Shape dough into walnut-sized balls. Roll in coconut flakes and place on parchment-lined baking sheets, leaving 2 inches between cookies.

Bake 10–12 minutes until bottom of cookies are slightly golden. Remove from oven and immediately press the reserved cherry halves into the center of each cookie.

Cool on cookie sheet for 5 minutes, then remove and cool completely on a wire rack.

Candy Bar Pretzel Cookies

(Submitted by Kay Garrett)
 Serves: Yield: 36 (3) inch cookies (yield may vary)

Ingredients:

2 cups all-purpose flour
1 teaspoon baking powder
½ teaspoon baking soda
1 teaspoon salt
1 cup butter, softened
1 cup light brown sugar
1 cup granulated sugar
⅔ cup smooth peanut butter
2 teaspoons pure vanilla extract
2 large eggs
1 (11 oz.) bag Snickers bars or Baby Ruth bars, cubed
1 cup chopped pretzels
1 cup cocktail peanuts, roughly chopped
1 cup milk-chocolate chips

Directions:

Preheat the oven to 350 degrees. Line two baking sheets with parchment paper.
 Sift together the all-purpose flour, baking powder, baking soda, and salt. Set aside.
 In the bowl of a stand mixer, cream together the softened butter, light brown sugar, granulated sugar, peanut butter, and vanilla. Beat for 3 minutes until smooth, fluffy, and light beige in color. Add the eggs one at a time, beating well after each

addition. Stop to scrape the bowl periodically so all the ingredients fully combine.

Add the dry ingredients gradually while beating on low speed, mixing well between each addition.

Repeat until all the dry ingredients have been added, stopping to scrape the sides of the bowl as needed.

After all the dry ingredients have been added, increase the speed of the mixer and beat for one minute.

Use a large nonstick spatula to mix the cubed Snickers bars, pretzels, peanuts, and chocolate chips into the batter by hand. The batter will be stiff. Mix until the ingredients are evenly distributed.

Use a 2- or 4-oz. ice-cream scoop to separate the dough, depending on the size you prefer. Place the dough rounds at least 3 inches apart on the baking sheet to allow room to spread. Press the centers to flatten slightly for even baking.

Bake for 18 minutes, rotating the pans if needed, until golden.

Cool on the cookie sheet for 5 minutes, then remove to a cooling rack to cool completely.

Chocolate Almond Coconut Cookies

(Submitted by Kay Garrett)

Ingredients:

1 cup butter
1 ½ cups white sugar
1 ½ cups brown sugar
4 eggs
3 teaspoons vanilla
4 ½ cups flour
2 teaspoons baking soda
1 teaspoon salt
5 cups chocolate chips
2 cups sweetened coconut
2 cups chopped almonds

Directions:

Preheat oven to 375 degrees. Lightly grease cookie sheets.
Combine dry ingredients, set aside.
In a large bowl, cream the butter and sugars together. Beat in the eggs, one at a time, stir in the vanilla. Stir in the dry ingredients until well mixed, then stir in the chocolate chips, coconut, and almonds. Drop by rounded full tablespoons onto the prepared cookie sheets.
Bake for 8 to 10 minutes. Cool on baking sheet for 5 minutes before removing to a wire rack to cool completely.

Mary's Sugar Cookies

(Submitted by Pat Davis)

Ingredients:

1 cup granulated sugar
1 cup powdered sugar
1 cup softened butter
2 eggs
1 cup vegetable oil
2 teaspoons vanilla
4 cups flour
1 teaspoon baking soda
1 teaspoon salt
1 teaspoon cream of tarter

Directions:

Cream together sugars, butter, and eggs.
Add vegetable oil and vanilla.
Mix together flour, baking soda, salt, and cream of tartar. Add to the other ingredients and mix until well-blended.
Separate into 2 parts, wrap in plastic wrap, and refrigerate overnight.
Take out 1 part at a time and roll in teaspoon-sized balls, roll in sugar, crisscross top with a fork.
Bake at 350 degrees for approximately six minutes.
Makes about 100 cookies.

Chocolate Crinkle Cookies

(Submitted by Alisha Collins)

Ingredients:

½ cup (2.2 oz/60 g) unsweetened cocoa powder
1 cup (7 oz/205 g) white granulated sugar
¼ cup (60ml) vegetable oil
2 large eggs
2 teaspoons pure vanilla extract
1 cup (3.5oz/130g) all purpose or plain flour
1 teaspoon baking powder
½ teaspoon salt
¼ cup confectioners' sugar or icing sugar (for coating)

Directions:

In a medium-sized bowl, mix together the cocoa powder, white sugar, and vegetable oil. Beat in eggs one at a time until fully incorporated. Mix in the vanilla.

In another bowl, combine the flour, baking powder, and salt. Stir the dry ingredients into the wet mixture just until a dough forms (do not overbeat). Cover bowl with wrap and refrigerate for at least 4 hours or overnight.

When ready to bake, preheat oven to 350 degrees F | 175 degrees C. Line 2 cookie sheets or baking trays with parchment paper (baking paper). Roll 1 tablespoonful of dough into balls for smaller cookies, or 2 tablespoonfuls for larger cookies.

Add the confectioners' (icing) sugar to a smaller bowl. Generously and evenly coat each ball of dough in confectioners' sugar and place onto prepared cookie sheets.

Bake in preheated oven for 10 minutes (for small cookies)

or 12 minutes (for larger cookies). The cookies will come out soft from the oven but will harden up as they cool.

Allow to cool on the cookie sheet for 5 minutes before transferring to wire racks to cool.

Applesauce Cookies

(Submitted by Valerie Peterson)

Ingredients:

½ cup butter
½ cup brown sugar
½ cup sugar
1 egg
1 teaspoon baking soda
1 cup applesauce
2 cups flour
½ teaspoon cloves
½ teaspoon salt
½ teaspoon cinnamon
1 teaspoon nutmeg

Directions:

Cream margarine, sugars, and eggs.
Add baking soda and applesauce.
Add dry ingredients.
Drop by teaspoon on greased cookie sheet.
Bake 8-10 minutes at 425.

Chocolate-Dipped Shortbread

(Submitted by Alisha Collins)

Ingredients:

1 cup salted butter, cold and cut up into pieces
2/3 cup granulated sugar
1 teaspoon almond extract (if you'd prefer the nut taste to be milder, use vanilla extract)
½ cup pecan pieces (I put mine in the food processor to get them nice and small)
2 ¼ cups all-purpose flour
½ cup Nutella
¼ cup semisweet chocolate chips
2 tablespoons milk
1 tablespoon confectioners' sugar

Directions:

In the bowl of an electric mixer, cream butter and sugar. Add in almond (or vanilla) extract. When these ingredients are well blended, add pecan pieces.

Gradually add flour and mix at low speed until combined, then increase speed to medium until your dough is no longer sandy-looking.

Put a piece of parchment paper on a baking tray, and turn dough out of mixing bowl. Divide in half. Form each half into a rectangle. I use my thumb as a width guide. Cover with plastic wrap and chill for 1 hour.

Preheat oven to 350 degrees.

Unwrap dough and use a pizza cutter to cut into sticks. Keep sticks close together on tray so they don't spread.

Bake in preheated oven for 15-20 minutes or until shortbread is golden and semi-firm to the touch.

Cool completely.

Over a double boiler, melt the semisweet chocolate chips, milk, sugar, and Nutella until smooth. You can also use a glass bowl in the microwave. Just make sure the chocolate doesn't burn.

Dip your shortbread sticks into the chocolate-Nutella mixture. Let cookies harden on parchment paper or just gobble them up there and then.

Ethyl's Chocolate Fudge

(Submitted by Erica Younce)

Ingredients:

4 cups sugar
1 cup milk
½ cup cocoa
1 cup evaporated milk
3 tablespoons butter
1 teaspoon vanilla

Directions:

Mix sugar, cocoa, and milk; mix well, then add evaporated milk.
Boil until mixture is set when dropped into cold water.
Add butter and vanilla.
Sit cooker down in a sink of cold water and beat until it starts getting thick.
Pour into 9-inch square pan. Cut into squares. Enjoy!

Sugar Cakes

(Submitted by Penny Lee Barton)

Ingredients:

½ lb. butter
2 cups sugar
3 eggs
1 tablespoon vanilla or lemon extract
4 cups flour
2 teaspoons baking powder
1 cup sour milk (1 cup milk + 1 tablespoon vinegar)
1 ½ teaspoons baking soda
½ teaspoon cream of tarter

Directions:

Mix all liquid ingredients except milk.
Mix milk and vinegar and set aside for 5 minutes.
Add dry ingredients, then sour milk. Mix well.
Drop by teaspoon on greased cookie sheet.
Bake at 350 degrees for 10 minutes.

Buttercream Candy

(Submitted by Colleen Galster)

Ingredients:

1 lb. 10x sugar
¼ lb. butter
1 tablespoon evaporated milk
1 teaspoon vanilla
Pinch of salt
Semisweet chocolate chips

Directions:

Mix all ingredients (except the chocolate chips) until it no longer sticks to your hands. If it does, add a little more 10x sugar until it no longer sticks.

Form into balls or whatever shape you choose, then place on a tray. Refrigerate for at least an hour until the buttercream is hardened some.

Melt the chocolate and coat the buttercream. Place back in the refrigerator until ready to serve. Keep refrigerated is best.

Black Walnut Cookies

(Submitted by Jeannie Daniel)

Ingredients:

1 cup butter, softened
2 cups packed brown sugar
2 eggs
1 tablespoon molasses
1 teaspoons vanilla
3 ½ cups all-purpose flour
1 teaspoon baking soda
¼ teaspoon salt
2 cups chopped black walnuts, divided

Directions:

Cream the butter and brown sugar together, beat in eggs, and vanilla. Combine flour, baking soda, and salt.
Gradually add the dry to the egg mixture. Stir in 1 ¼ cup walnuts. Finely chop the remaining nuts.
Shape dough into two 15-inch-long logs.
Roll the logs in the chopped nuts, pressing gently. Wrap in plastic wrap or towel. Refrigerate for 2 hours.
Unwrap and cut into ¼-inch slices. Place 2 inches apart on greased cookie sheets.
Bake at 300 degrees for 12 minutes. Cool. Makes about 10 dozen cookies.

Sunflower Refrigerator Cookies

(Submitted by Valerie Peterson)

Ingredients:

½ cup butter
½ cup brown sugar
1 teaspoon vanilla
¾ cup whole wheat flour
¼ cup wheat germ
¼ teaspoon salt
½ teaspoon baking soda
¾ cup dry-roasted sunflower seeds
½ cup sugar
1 egg
1 ½ cup quick oatmeal

Directions:

Cream butter and sugars. Add egg. Beat well.
Stir together dry ingredients, then add to creamed mixture.
Add sunflower seeds.
Divide dough into 2 rolls and wrap in wax paper. Chill at least 4 hours.
Cut into ¼ slices.
Bake at 375 degrees for 10–12 minutes or until lightly browned.

Pretzel Chocolate Bites

(Submitted by Cecile VanTyne)

Ingredients:

Mini pretzels
Rolo candy
Christmas M&M's

Directions:

Preheat the oven to 200 degrees.

On a cookie sheet, lay down as many pretzels as you'd like to make and put a Rolo on top of each one.

Bake for about 5 min until soft, remove from the oven, and put an M&M on each one.

Let them sit until they firm up and enjoy!

Ethyl's Oatmeal Raisin Cookies

(Submitted by Bea Tackett)

Ingredients:

1 cup soft shortening
1 ½ cups sugar
2 eggs
½ cup buttermilk
1 ¾ cups flour
1 teaspoon baking soda
1 teaspoon baking powder
½ teaspoon salt
1 teaspoon cinnamon
2 cups rolled oats
1 cup raisins, cut up
½ cup raisins, chopped

Directions:

Mix thoroughly: shortening, sugar, and eggs.
Stir in buttermilk
Sift together and stir in flour, baking soda, baking powder, salt, and cinnamon.
Stir in rolled oats, raisins, nuts.
Drop rounded teaspoons 2 inches apart on ungreased baking sheet.
Bake at 400 degrees for 8–10 minutes or until lightly browned.
Makes 5 ½ doz.

Goldbricks

(Submitted by Jan Knight)

Ingredients:

1 angel food cake mix OR your favorite scratch recipe
1 recipe of your favorite vanilla buttercream OR store bought
Salted peanuts -fined chopped (either salted in the shell OR canned)

Directions:

Bake the angel food as directed in a large loaf pan (16-inches long x 4 ½ inches wide x 4 inches high OR 2 regular 9 x 5 loaf pans.)
Bake as directed & let cool.
Cut the cake into small logs 4 by 1 ½-inch square.
Frost on all sides & roll in finely chopped peanuts (easier with 2 people - one to frost, one to roll in nuts).
Store in cool place or refrigerator with wax paper between layers OR freeze.
These actually get better with age!

Lemon Blueberry Scones

(Submitted by Shelia Hall)

Ingredients:

2 cups (250g) all-purpose flour (spoon & leveled), plus more for hands and work surface
6 tablespoons (75g) granulated sugar
1 tablespoon fresh lemon zest (about 1 lemon)
2 and ½ teaspoons baking powder
½ teaspoon salt
½ cup (1 stick; 115g) unsalted butter, frozen
½ cup (120ml) heavy cream (plus 2 Tbsp for brushing)
1 large egg
1 and ½ teaspoons pure vanilla extract
1 heaping cup (180g) fresh or frozen blueberries (do not thaw)
for topping: coarse sugar

Lemon Icing

1 cup (120g) confectioners' sugar
3 tablespoons fresh lemon juice (about 1 large lemon)

Directions:

Whisk flour, sugar, lemon zest, baking powder, and salt together in a large bowl. Grate the frozen butter using a box grater. Add it to the flour mixture and combine with a pastry cutter, two forks, or your fingers until the mixture comes together in pea-sized crumbs. Place in the refrigerator or freezer as you mix the wet ingredients together.

Whisk ½ cup heavy cream, the egg, and vanilla extract together in a small bowl. Drizzle over the flour mixture, add the blueberries, then mix together until everything appears moistened.

Pour onto the counter and, with floured hands, work dough into a ball as best you can. Dough will be sticky. If it's too sticky, add a little more flour. If it seems too dry, add 1 or 2 more tablespoons heavy cream. Press into an 8-inch disk and, with a sharp knife or bench scraper, cut into 8 wedges.

Brush scones with remaining heavy cream, and for extra crunch, sprinkle with coarse sugar. (You can do this before or after refrigerating in the next step.)

Place scones on a plate or lined baking sheet (if your fridge has space!) and refrigerate for at least 15 minutes.

Meanwhile, preheat oven to 400 degrees (204 degrees C).

Line a large baking sheet with parchment paper or silicone baking mat. After refrigerating, arrange scones 2 to 3 inches apart on the prepared baking sheet(s).

Bake for 22–25 minutes or until golden brown around the edges and lightly browned on top. Remove from the oven and cool for a few minutes before topping with lemon icing.

Make the icing: Whisk the icing ingredients together. Drizzle over warm scones.

Leftover iced or un-iced scones keep well at room temperature for 2 days or in the refrigerator for 5 days.

Chocolate Sandwich Cheesecake Cookies

(Submitted by Shelia Hall)

Ingredients:

1 8-ounce package cream cheese, softened
2 sticks butter, softened
1 ½ cups sugar
2 cups flour
20 chocolate sandwich cookies, coarsely chopped

Directions:

In a large bowl, beat cream cheese, butter, and sugar using a hand mixer or stand mixer until well blended. This should take a couple of minutes. You could use a whisk to do this by hand, just expect an intense arm workout.
Slowly add flour and mix until fully incorporated.
Gently fold in cookies. (I got a little too happy chopping my cookies, so they might be a bit more speckled with crumbs than yours.)
Cover your bowl with plastic wrap and chill the cookie dough in the fridge for at least 30 minutes. Chilling the dough is key here! The fat in the dough needs to solidify a bit to hold their shape while baking.
When you're ready to bake, preheat your oven to 350 degrees. On a cookie sheet lined with parchment paper, roll dough into balls using a cookie scoop (or 2 Tbsp. per cookie). Gently press the dough down with the back of a spoon to make a cookie shape. Tip: spray the spoon with nonstick spray first to prevent sticking.

Bake 12–15 minutes or until the edges are lightly brown and the center is puffed up. Let them cool on the pan for 5 minutes before cooling completely on a wire rack.

Peanut Butter Muffins

(Submitted by Jennifer Schmidt)

Ingredients:

1 bag Reese's miniature peanut butter cups
½ cup margarine
½ cup brown sugar
½ cup sugar
1 egg
1 teaspoon vanilla
½ cup creamy peanut butter
1 ½ cups flour
¾ teaspoon baking soda

Directions:

Spray or grease mini muffin pans or use mini cupcake papers.
Roll dough into small balls and place into muffin tins.
Bale for 8–9 minutes at 375 degrees.
Remove from oven; immediately put a peanut butter cup in the middle of each and push down.
Let cool.

Snowballs

(Submitted by Petrenia Etheridge)

Ingredients:

1 stick salted butter, softened
½ cup brown sugar
1 cup all-purpose flour
1 teaspoon ground cinnamon
1 teaspoon vanilla
½ cup finely chopped walnuts
Confectioners' sugar for rolling

Directions:

Cream butter, sugar, and cinnamon.
Add in flour and vanilla, mix well.
Stir in walnuts and a tablespoon of water, if necessary.
Use a teaspoon-size amount and roll into balls.
Place on greased cookie sheet or parchment paper.
Bake at 300 degrees for approximately 25 min.
Let cool to slightly warm and roll in confectioners' sugar.
Roll a second time if desired to make them nice and snowy.

Rudolph's Oatmeal Cookies

(Submitted by Brenda Ellis)

Ingredients:

1 cup butter, room temperature
1 cup brown sugar
½ cup granulated sugar
2 eggs
1 teaspoon vanilla
1 ½ cups all-purpose flour
1 teaspoon baking soda
1 teaspoon cinnamon
½ tsp salt
3 cups old-fashioned oats
1 cup fresh cranberries, quartered
1 cup pecans, chopped
1 cup white chocolate chips

Directions:

Preheat oven to 350 degrees.
Cream together butter and sugars until creamy.
Mix in eggs one at a time, then mix in vanilla.
In a separate bowl, whisk together flour, baking soda, cinnamon, and salt.
Add the flour mixture to the butter/sugar mixture and mix well.
Stir in oats, cranberries, pecans, and white-chocolate chips.
Drop about 1 tablespoon of dough on cookie sheet, leaving 2 inches between.

Bake 10–12 minutes or until edges start to brown. Cool on a cooling rack.

Recipes from Starlight at Moonglow

❄

Deborah Garner

Excerpt from *Starlight at Moonglow*

Whenever Betty hosted her yearly cookie exchange, Mist made a point of staying in the background. It was only fair to let Betty shine. She'd started the annual event long before Mist came to Timberton.

"How do I look?" Betty turned in a circle as Mist took in the hotelkeeper's attire. Her black wool gabardine skirt and low-heeled dress shoes were paired with a red sweater that featured a cheerful Santa Claus face, its swirling white beard heavily embellished with beads and sequins.

"Absolutely beautiful!" Mist said. "Has Clive seen you yet?"

Betty shook her head. "No, but I suspect he'll be around before long. Where there are cookies, there's Clive."

"Indeed." Mist laughed. "You can count on that."

"Oh! I hear the front door!" Betty's face lit up. "Let's see who's brought what!"

Enchanted by Betty's enthusiasm, Mist followed her out to the café, where dining tables had been brought together to form one long row. Floral centerpieces sat at regular intervals down the middle, leaving the rest of the surface free for platters of baked delights.

A stack of circular wire baskets waited at one end, an assortment of oversized quilting squares beside them. Betty had been thrilled with the idea of the basket and fabric combination as Mist collected remnants during the course of the year. Half the squares featured holiday patterns—holly branches, snowflakes, candy canes—while others boasted a variety of designs to use anytime of the year. Participants could line their baskets with whichever whimsical prints spoke to them, something to keep for the future.

Santa's Favorite Chocolate Cookies

(Submitted by Kim Davis of Cinnamon and Sugar and a Little Bit of Murder blog)

Ingredients:

1-¼ cups unsalted butter, room temperature
2 cups granulated sugar
2 eggs, room temperature
1 tablespoon pure vanilla extract
½ teaspoon espresso powder (or instant coffee)
¾ cup Dutch cocoa powder
2 cups all-purpose flour
1 teaspoon baking soda
1 teaspoon salt
*Coarse white sugar or peppermint crunch baking chips for garnish

Directions:

In a medium bowl, sift together the cocoa powder, all-purpose flour, baking soda, and salt. Set aside.
In the bowl of a standing mixer, beat the butter and sugar together until creamy, about 3 minutes.
Beat in the eggs, one at time, until fully incorporated. Mix in the vanilla.
Slowly add the dry ingredients to the butter and sugar mixture. Mix just until fully incorporated.
Separate the dough into two pieces and roll each piece into 12-inch logs (about 2 inches in diameter). Tightly wrap each log in parchment paper.
Refrigerate for at least 2 hours or overnight.

Preheat the oven to 350 degrees.

Slice the cookies into ½-inch-thick rounds and place on a parchment-lined baking sheet. Sprinkle tops of cookies with coarse white sugar or peppermint crunch baking chips.

Bake for 10 minutes, rotating pan once halfway through baking cycle.

Allow to cool on the baking sheet for 5 minutes, then remove to a wire rack to cool completely.

Store in an airtight container at room temperature for up to three days.

Tips: If dough is too hard to slice through, allow to sit at room temperature for 15–30 minutes.

The dough can be made up to 3 months ahead of time, formed into logs, and wrapped in parchment paper. Place the logs into a freezer-safe plastic bag and freeze until needed. Allow the frozen dough to defrost overnight in the refrigerator, then proceed as directed for slicing and baking.

Eggnog Cookie with Rum Butter Icing

(Submitted by Jeannie Daniel)

Ingredients:

1 stick unsalted butter, softened
1 cup dark brown sugar, packed
1 large egg
2/3 cup eggnog
2 cups flour
½ teaspoon baking soda
½ teaspoon salt
½ teaspoon nutmeg
½ teaspoon ginger
Nutmeg for garnish, optional

Directions:

Preheat oven to 350 degrees.
Cream butter, brown sugar, until creamy. Add in egg, mix, then add eggnog.
In a separate bowl, combine all the dry ingredients. Sift or whisk to mix well.
Add dry ingredients to eggnog mixture. Mix well.
Scoop a level ¼ cup measure and place on greased cookie sheet 2 inches apart.
Bake for 15 minutes.
When the cookies are cooled, mix ¼ cup butter, 1-½ cups powdered sugar, and 3 tablespoons rum or 2 tablespoons rum extract.
Melt the butter in a saucepan, then transfer to a bowl with the rum.

Stir in powdered sugar, ½ cup at a time, blending each addition until smooth.

Set it aside to thicken a little bit and spread into cooled cookies.

Dust with nutmeg or cinnamon to decorate.

These keep well in a tight-fitting container. They can also be refrigerated.

Apple Pie Cookies

(Submitted by Carol Anderson)

Ingredients:

½ cup shortening or butter
1 cup coconut sugar
1 egg substitute
1 teaspoon vanilla extract
½ cup apple, chopped fine
1 cup all-purpose flour
¼ cup wheat flour
½ teaspoon sea salt
2 teaspoons baking powder

Directions:

Cream sugar and shortening. Add egg substitute, vanilla, and apples.
Mix dry ingredients together and add to above.
Scoop by tablespoon, roll into balls, roll in sugar mix.
Bake at 350 degrees for 10–12 minutes.

Cherry Scones

(Submitted by Kris Bock from The Southwest Armchair Traveler blog)

Ingredients:

½ cup dried cherries, cranberries, or currents
½ apple juice or grape juice
2 cups flour
¼ cup sugar
½ teaspoon baking soda
2 teaspoons baking powder
½ teaspoon salt
½ teaspoon nutmeg
¼ cup cold butter
1 egg
½ cup plain yogurt (full-fat preferred)
1 teaspoon lemon or orange zest

Directions:

Preheat oven to 375 degrees.
Soak cherries in juice for at least 10 minutes while you mix other ingredients.
Mix the flour and ¼ cup of the sugar. Blend in the baking soda, baking powder, salt, and nutmeg.
Cut in the butter with a pastry blender or two knives until the mixture has fine crumbs.
Stir in the egg, yogurt, and zest. Drain the cherries or other dried fruit well. Mix them in.
Spray a baking sheet lightly with oil.

More Sweet Treats

Turn the dough onto the baking sheet. Pat it down into a 9-inch circle.

Cut the dough into 8 wedges. Separate them slightly. You may sprinkle with additional sugar if you want them to sparkle a bit.

Bake until golden and firm, about 20 minutes.

Serve warm with butter, clotted cream, orange marmalade, or jam.

*This recipe also works well with dried cranberries or currents.

Aunt Nellie's PB Surprise

(Submitted by Petrenia Etheridge)

Ingredients:

Ritz crackers
Peanut butter
Marshmallows

Directions:

Spread peanut butter on Ritz crackers, salt side down, and place on cookie sheet about 2 inches apart. Add a marshmallow to the top of each.
Bake at 350 degrees until marshmallows swell and are lightly brown.
Remove from oven and let them deflate. Serve with hot cocoa while still warm.

Christmas Snow Clouds

(Submitted by Petrenia Etheridge)
  (Cream cheese teacake puffs)

Ingredients:

1 egg
½ cup salted butter
4 oz. cream cheese
½-1 cup sugar, depends on desired sweetness
1-¼ cups cake flour
½ teaspoon baking powder
1 teaspoon vanilla extract
1 teaspoon rum, almond or lemon extract

Directions:

Make sure first 3 ingredients are room temperature. Cream together butter and cream cheese until well blended, then add sugar and blend well.

Add in egg and extracts until well incorporated. Fork cake flour and baking powder separately, then add slowly and blend gently. Chill mixture 1–2 hours.

Preheat oven to 375 degrees and line baking sheet with parchment paper. Spoon 1–2-inch balls into paper with a floured spoon. Slightly press with a floured cup but not flat or they won't puff up.

Bake for 8-10 minutes until bottoms are slightly brown. Decorate with your favorite icing when cool or just top with confectioners' sugar or sprinkles.

Whipped Chocolate Chip Shortbread Cookies

(Submitted by Shelia Hall)

Ingredients:

1 cup butter, room temperature
1-½ cups all-purpose flour
½ cup powdered sugar
1 cup chocolate chips

Directions:

In a mixing bowl, (or bowl from stand mixer) on low-speed blend butter, all-purpose flour, and icing sugar for 1 minute.
Increase speed to medium and mix for seven minutes.
Add in chocolate chips by hand, mixing only until combined, being gentle when mixing.
Using a cookie scoop or heaping tablespoon, drop onto baking sheets 12 to a sheet.
Bake at 350 degrees for 10-12 minutes until edges are just light golden brown, being careful not to overbake.
Remove from oven and cool at least five minutes before transferring to a wire cooling rack.
Store cookies in an airtight container for up to five days or in refrigerator container for up to ten days.

Sugar-Free Orange Cookies

(Submitted by Brenda Ellis)

Ingredients:

1 ½ cups all-purpose flour
1 teaspoon baking powder
Sugar substitute equal to ¾ cup sugar
2 teaspoons grated orange zest
¼ teaspoon salt
⅛ teaspoon ground nutmeg
½ cup vegetable oil spread
⅓ cup chopped golden raisins
¼ cup egg substitute
2 tablespoons orange juice

Directions:

Combine first six ingredients. Cut in spread until mixture resembles coarse crumbs.
Stir in raisins.
Add egg substitute and orange juice.
Mix well.
Drop by teaspoonfuls onto baking sheet coated with cooking spray.
Flatten with a fork coated with flour.
Bake at 375 degrees for 13–15 minutes.
Remove and let cool on cooling rack.

Cranberry White Chocolate Bars

(Submitted by Molly Elliott)

Ingredients:

2 large eggs
½ teaspoon vanilla extract
1 cup sugar
1 cup all-purpose flour
¼ teaspoon salt
½ cup butter, melted
¾ cups fresh or frozen (thawed) cranberries, coarsely chopped
½ (11-oz) bag white chocolate chips

Directions:

Preheat oven to 350 degrees.
Whisk together eggs and vanilla extract in a mixing bowl until blended.
Gradually add sugar, beating until blended.
Stir in flour, salt, and melted butter.
Gently stir in cranberries and white chocolate chips.
Spread dough in a lightly greased 8-inch square pan.
Bake 38 to 40 minutes or until a toothpick inserted in center comes out clean.
Cool and cut into bars.

Rhubarb Cookies

(Submitted by Brenda Brodmerkel)

Ingredients:

1 cup butter, softened
2 eggs
1 cup sugar
½ cup brown sugar
2 teaspoons vanilla extract
2-½ cups flour
1 teaspoon baking powder
½ teaspoon salt

Directions:

Preheat oven to 400 degrees.

In mixing bowl, cream together with 2 eggs, 1 cup soft butter, 1 cup sugar, ½ cup brown sugar, and 2 teaspoons vanilla.

Mix in separate bowl 2-½ cups flour, 1 tsp. baking powder, ½ tsp. salt.

Add to wet mixture.

Add 1 cup white choc chips and 2 cups cut-up rhubarb.

Drop by spoonful onto baking sheet and bake for 14 minutes.

Cherry Brownie Bon Bons

(Submitted by Vera Kenyon)

Ingredients:

1 fudge brownie mix
¼ cup Kirschwasser / cherry brandy or ¼ cup water
¼ cup vegetable oil
1 egg
2 10 oz. jars maraschino cherries with stems
½ cup powdered sugar

Chocolate Fudge Filling

1 3 oz. pkg cream cheese
1 teaspoon vanilla
¼ cup light corn syrup
3 squares of unsweetened chocolate, melted and cooled
1 cup powdered sugar

Directions:

Preheat oven to 350 degrees.
Stir brownie mix, Kirschwasser, oil, and egg in a bowl 50 strokes until well blended.
Fill greased, miniature muffin cups two-thirds full of brownie batter.
Bake for 15 minutes or until a wooden toothpick comes out with fudgy crumbs. Be careful not to overbake.
Cool slightly and remove from the muffin pans. While the brownies are still warm, put them on a waxed-paper-lined tray.

Make a half-inch indentation into each brownie with the end of a wooden spoon. Cool completely.

Prepare the chocolate fudge filling. For the filling, beat cream cheese and vanilla in a small bowl. Slowly pour in the corn syrup, then add chocolate and beat until smooth. Gradually add the powdered sugar and blend well.

When the filling is prepared, drain the cherries, reserving the liquid. Let the cherries sit on a paper towel to dry.

Combine the powdered sugar with enough reserved liquid to form a thin glaze.

Spoon or pipe about one teaspoon of the chocolate fudge into the indentation of each brownie.

Gently press a cherry into the filling. Drizzle with the sugar glaze.

Impossible Peanut Butter Cookies

(Submitted by Mary Elizabeth Terberg)

Ingredients:

1 cup creamy peanut butter
1 cup sugar
1 egg
1 teaspoon vanilla

Directions:

Mix all ingredients together.
Drop by spoonful on ungreased cookie sheet.
Press each cookie with a fork greased with butter and dipped in sugar.
Bake at 325 degrees for 10–12 minutes.
Let cool on cookie sheet.
Makes 18.

Caramel Popcorn Balls

(Submitted by Betty Escobar)

Ingredients:

1 cup butter
1 cup brown sugar
½ cup light corn syrup
2/3 cup (½ 15 oz. can) sweetened condensed milk
½ teaspoon vanilla
5 quarts popcorn

Directions:

In saucepan, combine all ingredients except condensed milk and vanilla.
Bring to boil over medium heat, stirring well.
Stir in condensed milk and simmer, stirring constantly, until it reaches soft ball stage (234–238).
Stir in vanilla.
Pour over popcorn and mix. Butter hands and form into balls approximately 3-½ inches.
Makes 15.

Mom's Angel Pie

(Submitted by Pat Decoster)

Ingredients:

8 eggs, separated into whites and yolks
3 cups sugar separated into 2 cup and 1 cup portions
1 teaspoon cream of tartar
¼ cup lemon juice

Directions:

Beat 8 egg whites until frothy.
Slowly add 2 cups of sugar and cream of tartar.
Spread into 9 x 13-inch pan and bake at 300 degrees for 20 minutes.
Turn oven down to 250 degrees and bake another 40 minutes.
Beat 8 egg yolks well with 1 cup sugar and lemon juice. Cook in double broiler until thick.
Allow to cool, then spread over bottom layer and cover with whipped cream or Cool Whip.

Amish Sugar Cookies

(Submitted by Alma Collins)

Ingredients:

4-½ cups all-purpose flour
1 teaspoon baking soda
1 teaspoon salt
1 cup sugar
1 cup powdered sugar
2 eggs
1 cup oil
1 cup butter
1 teaspoon vanilla

Directions:

Mix together flour, baking soda, and salt, and set aside.
Cream together sugar, powdered sugar, eggs, oil, butter, and vanilla. Add flour mixture.
Roll into balls and place on an ungreased cookie sheet.
Grease bottom of glass or cookie stamp and dip into sugar to press cookie.
Bake at 350 degrees for 8–10 minutes. (Hint: Use seasonal cookie stamps and colored sugar.)

Grinch Cookies

(Submitted by Shelly Maynard)

Makes 24 cookies
Prep time: 10 minutes
Bake time: 9 minutes
Frosting time: 10 minutes

Ingredients:

1 box of white cake mix
2 large eggs
½ cup vegetable oil
1 cup powdered sugar
1 tablespoon milk
1 teaspoon vanilla
Green food coloring
Yellow food coloring
Red heart sprinkles

Directions:

Preheat the oven to 350 degrees.
Line a baking sheet with parchment paper.
Add cake mix, eggs, and vegetable oil to a large bowl and stir well.
Add equal amounts of green and yellow food coloring to get your desired "Grinch" color, about 4 drops of each.
Using a cookie scoop, drop scoops of dough onto a baking sheet, 1–2 inches apart.
Bake for 9 minutes. Remove from the oven and set the baking sheet on a wire cooling rack for one minute.

More Sweet Treats

Remove cookies from the baking sheet onto the wire cooling rack. Allow cookies to cool completely.

Mix the powdered sugar, milk, and vanilla in a small bowl.

Add 2 drops each of green and yellow food coloring. Stir well.

Check the consistency. It should be just perfect—not too runny and not too thick.

Spread icing on the cookies.

Place a heart in the center of the cookies.

Chai Tea Shortbread Cookies

(Submitted by Kris Bock from The Southwest Armchair Traveler blog)

**If using loose-leaf tea, grind the tea into a rough powder first. If using tea bags, cut open the tea bags (4–6) and measure. Tea bags usually have a more powdered mix, so you don't have to grind it. Mix the ingredients in a food processor for ease. You can also press the dough into a shortbread pan and bake for about 30 minutes.

Ingredients:

2 cups all-purpose flour
2/3 cup sugar
2 tablespoons chai tea (ground fine)
½ teaspoon salt
1 cup (2 sticks) butter, room temperature
2 teaspoons vanilla extract

Directions:

Preheat oven to 375 degrees.
Blend the flour, sugar, chai, and salt.
Mix in the butter and vanilla. Press the mixture into a ball of dough.
Roll out the dough on a floured surface to about ⅓-inch thick. Use a cookie cutter and place cookies 2 inches apart on baking sheets lined with parchment paper or silicone baking sheets.
Bake until the edges are golden, 8–12 minutes depending on size.

Let cool on sheets for 5 minutes, then transfer to wire racks and cool to room temperature.

Nutella Hazelnut Brownies

(Submitted by Katie Brown)

Ingredients:

1 and ½ cup Nutella or hazelnut spread
½ cup flour
2 eggs
½ tablespoon olive oil
2 to 4 oz halved hazelnuts
¼ cup semi-sweet chocolate chips

Directions:

Preheat oven to 325 degrees.
Mix Nutella, flour, eggs, oil until well combined with beaters.
Stir in hazelnuts and chocolate chips. Spread into greased/olive oiled pan.
Bake 30 to 35 min until middle no longer jiggles when shaking the pan.
*For 8 x 8 glass pan, 38 minutes to get brownies still very moist and fudgy but cooked through.
Let cool slightly before serving or packaging individually.

Peanut Butter Chocolate Fudge

(Submitted by Lena Winfrey Hayat)

Ingredients:

20 reg. size peanut butter cups
3 cups of chocolate chips
14 oz. can sweetened condensed milk

Directions:

Put 16 peanut butter cups face down in a dish.

Mix milk and chocolate chips together. Microwave for 1 min. Stir and then microwave for another 3 to 5 min. until melted.

Pour mixture over peanut butter cups.

Break the last 4 peanut butter cups into pieces. Spread over top, gently pushing down into mixture.

Refrigerate until set. Cut into squares.

Christmas Dreams

(Submitted by Colleen Galster)

Ingredients:

15 oz. box white cake mix
2 large eggs
⅓ cup cream soda
½ cup butterscotch chips
½ cup white chocolate chips
Optional: sprinkles

Directions:

Preheat oven to 350 degrees and line cookie sheets with parchment paper.

Mix cake mix, eggs, and cream soda. Stir until fully combined.

Fold in butterscotch chips and white chocolate chips.

Scoop batter onto cookie sheets 2 inches apart. Add sprinkles if desired.

Bake for 8–10 minutes or until the middle sets and edges start to turn a light golden brown.

Let cool 10 minutes, then serve.

*Adapt with any flavor combination by choosing a different cake mix, clear soda, and mix-ins.

Recipes from Joy at Moonglow

❄

Deborah Garner

Excerpt from *Joy at Moonglow*

No matter how busy the holidays turned out to be, no one ever wanted to miss Betty's annual cookie exchange, and this year was no exception. It wasn't even the sugary treats themselves that brought people to the hotel bearing batches of cookies and platters of similar holiday goodies. Certainly, the thought of lush chocolate, vanilla, lemon, ginger, and peanut butter flavors helped lure participants as did the textures of royal icing, chopped nuts, and candy sprinkles. But it was tradition itself that topped the reasons the cookie exchange was always well attended. That and perhaps a chance to hear the latest scoop on town gossip - all well-meaning, of course.

There was also the draw of the containers provided each year, always unique and creative. Mist delighted in coming up with different containers each year that could be used to hold the mix-and-match variety of sweets that would go home with each person once everything had been shared. Regular participants had come to save the containers over the years, accumulating a collection to be reused or just enjoyed as is. Wooden boxes, glass jars, baskets, and small sleighs had all been used at one time or another. Each year was a little different, just as everything in Timberton was somehow unique each year.

Months before, while frequenting antique shops and thrift stores in surrounding areas, Mist came across a stack of four vintage pie plates on a late-summer afternoon. Shallow and circular with lovely, fluted edges, they seemed destined for a special holiday use. She'd purchased them all, and now, with intricate painted swirls of silver and gold around the outer glass, they waited at the end of the buffet in the Moonglow Cafe, ready to be filled with cookies and sweets.

Christmas Hugs and Kisses Cookies

(Submitted by Kim Davis of Cinnamon and Sugar and a Little Bit of Murder blog)

Ingredients:

1 cup all-purpose flour
½ cup unsweetened cocoa powder
½ teaspoon salt
½ cup unsalted butter, room temperature
2/3 cup granulated sugar
1 egg
½ teaspoon peppermint extract
¾ cup holiday-themed nonpareils and jimmies (use a mixture)
24 Hershey's Hugs and Kisses candies, unwrapped (or a combination of the two)

Directions:

In a medium bowl, whisk together the "our, cocoa powder, and salt.
Using an electric mixer, beat the butter on medium-high speed until creamy.
Add in the sugar and beat for 2 minutes until light and fluffy.
Beat in the egg and the peppermint extract until thoroughly combined.
Refrigerate the dough for at least 30 minutes.
Preheat the oven to 350 degrees. Line two baking sheets with parchment paper and set aside.
Place the sprinkles in a shallow dish. Shape the dough into

balls about the size of a small walnut and roll in the sprinkles. Place on baking sheet at least 2 inches apart.

Bake cookies, one sheet at a time, for 10 to 11 minutes. Remove the pan from the oven and lightly press a Hugs and Kiss candy into the center of each cookie while they are warm.

Allow cookies to rest on baking sheet for 5 minutes, then remove to a wire rack to cool before eating.

Let Hugs and Kisses form up before storing in an airtight container for up to one week.

Tip:

Use different-colored sprinkles for other holidays and special occasions.

Peppermint Snowball Cookies

(Submitted by Shelia Hall)

Ingredients:

2 cups + 2 tablespoons all-purpose flour
2 teaspoon cornstarch
1 cup salted sweet cream butter softened
3 cups powdered sugar divided (2 cups and 1 cup)
1 teaspoon pure peppermint extract
½ teaspoon pure vanilla extract
1-¼ cup mini semisweet chocolate chips 5–6 drops hot pink/rose food color gel
¼ cup finely crushed peppermint candies

Directions:

Whisk together the flour and cornstarch. Set it aside.

Using either a stand mixer or a large mixing bowl and a handheld mixer on medium-high, beat the softened butter for 30 seconds. Add the 1 cup of powdered sugar and beat for another 1 to 1-½ minutes.

Lower the mixer speed to medium-low, add in the peppermint and vanilla extracts. Keeping the mixer speed on medium-low, add in the flour mixture. Mix just until the ingredients are well incorporated. Increase the mixer speed to medium and add the red food color. Mix just until the color is uniform.

Add in the mini chocolate chips and mix just until combined and well distributed. Cover the dough and chill in the refrigerator for 10 minutes.

Preheat the oven to 350 degrees. Line two baking sheets

with parchment paper, one for baking the dough balls and one for the rolled cookies to finish cooling on. Set them aside.

Using a 1 tablespoon cookie dough scoop, scoop out the cookie dough. Roll the dough into a ball and place on the prepared baking sheet. Space the rolled cookie dough balls 1 inch apart. Bake for 10–12 minutes.

Add the remaining 2 cups powdered sugar and the crushed peppermint candies to a medium-size mixing bowl. Whisk to combine. Set it aside.

Remove the cookies from the oven and allow them to rest on the cookie sheet for 5 minutes. Roll the cookies in the powdered sugar mixture. Transfer the coated cookies to the second prepared cookie sheet.

Peanut Butter Cocoa Drops

(Submitted by Shelia Hall)

Ingredients:

2 cups sugar
⅓ cup unsweetened cocoa powder
½ cup milk
1 stick of butter
1 teaspoon vanilla
Pinch of salt
½ cup peanut butter (chunky)
2 cups quick-cooking oats

Directions:

Combine the sugar, cocoa milk, and butter in a medium saucepan. Cook on medium heat until it comes to a boil, stirring occasionally.
Boil for 1 minute. Remove from heat and stir in the vanilla, salt, peanut butter, and oats.
Drop by rounded spoonfuls onto waxed paper or aluminum
foil.
Cool for around an hour, then store in an airtight container.

Gluten-Free Apple Cookies

(Submitted by Petrenia Etheridge)

Ingredients:

4 packets apple instant oatmeal
½ cup sugar
¼ cup butter, softened
1 tablespoon honey
1 teaspoon vanilla
½ teaspoon cinnamon
¼ teaspoon salt
1 large egg

Directions:

Cream together butter and sugar. Add in everything except oatmeal and mix well. Then stir in oatmeal and mix well.
Spoon onto greased cookie sheet by teaspoon size.
Bake at 350 degrees for 10 min. They will have a chewy texture. For crisper cookies, add ½ cup gluten-free flour.

No-Bake Gluten-Free Cookies

(Submitted by Petrenia Etheridge)

Ingredients:

½ cup butter
2 cup sugar
4 tablespoons cocoa
½ cup peanut butter
½ cup milk
1 tablespoon corn syrup
Pinch salt
1 teaspoon vanilla
3 cups quick oats

Directions:

In saucepan, melt butter. Add cocoa powder, sugar, salt, corn syrup, and milk. Stir until smooth.
Once boiling, boil for 2-½ minutes and remove from heat. Stir in peanut butter and vanilla, then fold in oats.
Spoon onto parchment paper to cool.

Raspberry Bars

(Submitted by Brenda Ellis)

Ingredients:

One box yellow cake mix
2-½ cups quick oats
¾ cup melted butter
12 oz. jar raspberry preserves

Directions:

Combine cake mix and oats. Stir in butter and mix until crumbly.
Press about 3 cups into a 9 x 13 pan.
Spread raspberry (or other fruit) preserves over mixture. Sprinkle remaining crumb mixture over preserves. Pat gently to level.
Bake at 375 degrees for 24–26 minutes. Cool completely and cut into bars.

Coconut Oatmeal Cookies

(Submitted by Linda Bye)

Ingredients:

1 cup of softened butter
¼ cup white sugar
¾ cup packed brown sugar
2 eggs
1 teaspoon baking soda
1 small package of coconut cream instant Jello pudding
1-¼ cup flour
1 cup old-fashioned oats
2-½ cups quick oats

Directions:

Blend together butter and sugars until smooth.
Add eggs, baking soda, and pudding package.
Mix in flour and all oats.
With a tablespoon, distribute dough on 2 nonstick 18 x 13 cookie sheets.
Bake 9–11 minutes at 375 degrees. Recipe makes approximately 48 cookies.
Optional add-ins: 1 cup Craisins
1 cup of semisweet chocolate chips

Hearty Banana Tea Loaves/Muffins

(Submitted by Jennifer Harvey)

Ingredients:

½ cup boiling water
1 cup rolled oats
1-½ cups mashed bananas (approximately 3 medium)
1 cup brown sugar
2 eggs
1 teaspoon vanilla
1-⅓ cups flour
2 teaspoons baking soda
¼ teaspoon salt

Directions:

Preheat oven to 350° for loaves or 400° for muffins.
Butter pans or dust with flour. Cupcake liners may be used to line muffin pans.
Pour boiling water over oats to soften. Let cool.
Mix bananas, sugar, eggs, and vanilla in a large mixing bowl. Add flour, soda, salt, and softened oats to banana mixture. Beat until smooth. Add batter to prepared pans.
Bake tea loaves for approximately 40 minutes at 350°.
Bake muffins for 15–25 minutes at 400 degrees.
Bread is done when inserted toothpick comes out clean.
Optional: Sprinkle tops with turbinado sugar and walnut pieces for a lovely crunch.

Double-Chocolate Lemon Cookies

(Submitted by Lanette Fields)

Ingredients:

2 sticks of butter or Earth Balance, softened
1 teaspoon vanilla
2 eggs or egg substitute
2 cups dark brown sugar, packed.
2/3 cup baking cocoa
3 cups of one-to-one gluten-free flour with xanthan gum
1-½ teaspoon baking soda
1 teaspoon of baking powder
1 bag of semisweet chocolate chips
Zest of one large lemon

Directions:

Preheat oven to 325 degrees on convection bake.
Sift together flour, cocoa, baking soda, and baking powder. Set aside.
Mix butter, sugar, eggs, and vanilla until well combined.
Add dry ingredients slowly to creamed mixture just until completely blended.
Add one bag of semisweet chocolate chips.
Add the zest of one large lemon.
Mix until incorporated.
Use cookie scoop or make cookie balls about size of walnuts.
Put on parchment-lined baking sheets about three fingers apart. Bake about 10 minutes or until desired doneness. Let

them cool on baking sheet or after one minute transfer to cooling racks to cool.

Makes about 43 cookies.

Tips: When cool, wrap cookies in plastic wrap and put in freezer bag to stay fresh longer. Can be stored in the freezer for about 6 months. Regular flour can be substituted for gluten-free flour and real butter for buttery sticks. Amount of flour and leveling may need to be adjusted. Use chocolate chips such as Guittard 46% Cacao chips for nondairy.

Mocha Peppermint Cookies

(Submitted by Colleen Galster)

Ingredients:

1 box gluten-free chocolate cake mix (I use King Arthur brand)
2 eggs
⅓ cup melted butter
1 teaspoon peppermint extract
2 teaspoons peppermint coffee creamer or other holiday flavors. You can use milk instead if you prefer.
1 cup semisweet chocolate chips
1 cup white chocolate chips
Peppermint baking chips or crushed candy canes optional
Butterscotch chips (optional)
Caramel syrup (optional)

Directions:

Preheat oven to 350 degrees.
In a large mixing bowl, add the eggs, and beat slightly.
Stir in the cake mix, melted butter, peppermint extract and coffee creamer or milk, and mix until well combined.
Stir in the chocolate and white chocolate chips.
Drop by rounded tablespoonful onto cookie sheet, leaving about 2 inches between cookies.
Place several peppermint chips/candy cane pieces and chocolate chips on top of each cookie.
Bake for 8 to 10 minutes or until edges are slightly warm. Remove from oven and allow to cool completely. Drizzle with caramel syrup if desired.

Cranberry Almond Scone Cookies

(Submitted by Molly Elliott)

Ingredients:

½ cup butter, softened (1 stick)
⅓ cup granulated sugar
⅓ cup brown sugar
1 teaspoon vanilla
1 egg (or egg replacer)
1 ½ cups all-purpose flour
½ teaspoon baking powder
¼ teaspoon baking soda
½ teaspoon salt
2 tablespoons milk
½ cup dried cranberries
½ cup sliced almonds

Directions:

Sift dry ingredients together and set aside.
Cream butter and sugar together. Add vanilla and egg (or egg replacer).
Add dry ingredients and milk. Mix well.
Add cranberries and sliced almonds (or additions of choice). Mix and drop by spoonful on greased baking sheet. Press cookies down slightly before putting in the oven. Bake approximately 10 minutes at 350 degrees.

Mexican Wedding Cakes

(Submitted by Betty Escobar)

Ingredients:

2 cups butter
1 cup confectioners' sugar (plus extra)
1 teaspoon vanilla
4 cups flour
1 cup finely chopped pecans

Directions:

Preheat oven to 350 degrees.
Cream butter and one cup confectioners' sugar until light and fluffy, 5–7 minutes. Beat in vanilla.
Gradually beat in flour and stir in pecans.
Shape tablespoons of dough into 2-inch crescents. Bake 12–15 minutes or until light brown.
Roll in additional confectioners' sugar while warm. Cool on wire racks.

Banana Oatmeal Cookies

(Submitted by M. J. McKinniss, from Gramma R.)

Ingredients:

½ cup sugar
½ cup brown sugar
2 eggs beaten
1 cup shortening
2 cups sifted flour
2 cups oatmeal—not cooked
1 cup mashed bananas
1 teaspoon baking soda
1 teaspoon vanilla
One bag of butterscotch chips (10 or 12 oz. bag)

Directions:

Sift flour into mixing bowl, add the rest of the ingredients and mix until well blended.

Add the entire bag of butterscotch chips or only as many as you'd like.

Bake at 375 degrees on a greased cookie sheet for about 12 minutes or until golden brown.

An alternate to the butterscotch chips:

My grandmother originally made these cookies with date fruits (pits removed). The batter for this cookie is thick, so you can take a date fruit, just one, and put it on the underside of the tablespoon or so of cookie dough, slightly pushing it into the dough (this would be the bottom of the cookie when done). I put the date on the cookie sheet, then put my blob of cookie dough on top of it and kind of form it around the date. The date will caramelize while baking.

Lila's Lace Cookies

(Submitted by Sallie Reynolds, from Lila Doggett)

Ingredients:

1 cup melted butter
2 cups brown sugar
1 large egg
1 teaspoon vanilla
1 cup pecan meats
2 cups rolled oats

Directions:

Mix in order given, place far apart on baking sheet, bake in moderate oven.
Note: Use the dull side of foil as a liner. Let the cookies cool thoroughly.
Moderate oven is between 350 and 375 degrees.

Holly Cookies

(Submitted by Betty Escobar)

Ingredients:

½ cup butter
30 large (not jumbo) marshmallows
½ teaspoon vanilla
1-½ teaspoons green food coloring
3-½ cups cornflakes
Red cinnamon candies

Directions:

In large pot, melt butter and marshmallows together, stirring constantly.
Add vanilla and food coloring.
Stir in cornflakes.
Drop spoonfuls with a greased spoon onto a greased cookie sheet or wax paper sprayed with vegetable oil.
Place 2 cinnamon candies on each bunch of holly, pressing lightly to make sure they stick. Let sit until they set.
Note: To make these gluten-free, make sure to use brands of marshmallows and cornflakes that are gluten-free.

Chocolate Waffle Cookies

(Submitted by Vera Kenyon)

Ingredients:

1-½ cups sugar
1 cup butter
4 eggs
2 teaspoons vanilla
2 cups flour
8 tablespoons cocoa
Dash of salt

Directions:

Cream sugar and butter. Beat in eggs and vanilla.
Mix in dry ingredients.
Place a spoonful of batter in each section of your waffle iron.
Bake a minute or two.
Remove the waffles, let cool and add frosting and sprinkles if you like.

Chocolate Crinkle Cookies

(Submitted by Alisha Collins)

Ingredients:

½ cup unsweetened cocoa powder
1 cup white granulated sugar
¼ cup vegetable oil
2 large eggs
2 teaspoons pure vanilla extract
1 cup all-purpose or plain flour
1 teaspoon baking powder
½ teaspoon salt
¼ cup confectioner's sugar or icing sugar (for coating)

Directions:

In a medium-sized bowl, mix together the cocoa powder, white sugar, and vegetable oil. Beat in eggs one at a time until fully incorporated. Mix in the vanilla.

In another bowl, combine the flour, baking powder, and salt. Stir the dry ingredients into the wet mixture just until a dough forms. Do not over beat.

Cover bowl with wrap and refrigerate for at least 4 hours or overnight.

When ready to bake, preheat oven to 350 degrees. Line 2 cookie sheets or baking trays with parchment paper.

Roll 1 tablespoonful of dough into balls for smaller cookies (or 2 tablespoonfuls for larger cookies).

Add the confectioners' sugar to a smaller bowl. Generously and evenly coat each ball of dough in confectioners' sugar and place onto prepared cookie sheets.

Bake in preheated oven for 10 minutes (for small cookies) or 12 minutes (for larger cookies). The cookies will come out soft from the oven but will harden up as they cool.

Let cool for 5 minutes before transferring to wire racks.

Easy Peanut Butter Cookies

(Submitted by Alisha Collins)

Ingredients:

1 cup peanut butter
1 cup sugar
1 egg

Directions:

Preheat oven to 350 degrees and spray your pan with nonstick spray.

Combine all ingredients and drop by spoonfuls onto baking pan. Use a fork dipped in sugar to make the crisscross pattern.

Bake for 6–8 minutes only! They will be soft and barely brown on the bottom.

Option: Add peanut butter chips or dark chocolate chips.

Chocolate-Dipped Shortbread Cookies

(Submitted by Alisha Collins)

Ingredients:

1 cup salted butter, cold and cut up into pieces
2/3 cup granulated sugar
1 teaspoon almond extract (if you'd prefer the nut taste to be milder, use vanilla extract)
½ cup pecan pieces (I put mine in the food processor to get them nice and small)
2-¼ cups all-purpose flour
½ cup Nutella
¼ cup semisweet chocolate chips
2 tablespoons milk
1 tablespoon confectioners' sugar

Directions:

In the bowl of an electric mixer, cream butter and sugar. Add in almond (or vanilla) extract. When these ingredients are well blended, add pecan pieces.

Gradually add flour and mix at low speed until combined, then increase speed to medium until your dough is no longer sandy-looking.

Put a piece of parchment paper on a baking tray and turn dough out of mixing bowl. Divide in half. Form each half into a rectangle. I use my thumb as a width guide. Cover with plastic wrap and chill for 1 hour.

Preheat oven to 350 degrees.

Unwrap dough and use a pizza cutter to cut into sticks. Keep sticks close together on tray so they don't spread.

Bake in preheated oven for 15–20 minutes or until shortbread is golden and semi-firm to the touch.

Cool completely.

Over a double boiler, melt the semisweet chocolate chips, milk, sugar, and Nutella until smooth. You can also use a glass bowl in the microwave. Just make sure the chocolate doesn't burn.

Dip your shortbread sticks into the chocolate-Nutella mixture. Let cookies harden on parchment paper or just gobble them up there and then.

Cranberry Orange Cookies

(Submitted by Patti Rusk)

Ingredients for cookie dough:

1 cup unsalted butter, softened
1 cup white sugar
½ cup packed brown sugar
1 large egg
2 tablespoons orange juice
1 teaspoon grated orange zest
2-½ cups all-purpose flour
½ teaspoon baking soda
½ teaspoon salt
2 cups chopped cranberries or Craisins
½ cup chopped walnuts

Glaze:
1-½ cups confectioners' sugar 3 tablespoons orange juice
½ teaspoon grated orange zest

Directions:

Preheat oven to 375 degrees.
Cream butter, white sugar, and brown sugar in a mixing bowl until smooth. Beat in egg until well blended. Mix in orange juice and zest.
Whisk together flour, baking soda, and salt in a separate bowl. Stir flour mixture into the butter mixture until combined. Mix in cranberries and walnuts.
Drop dough by rounded tablespoonfuls 2 inches apart onto ungreased cookie sheets.

More Sweet Treats

Bake in the preheated oven 11–14 minutes until edges are golden brown. Be sure to turn racks halfway through.

Cool cookies completely before adding glaze.

To make the glaze:

Mix together confectioners' sugar, orange juice, and zest in a small bowl until smooth.

Drizzle or spread glaze over the tops of the cooled cookies.

Let stand until set.

Raspberry Almond Cookies

(Submitted by Patti Rusk)

Ingredients:

1 cup butter, softened
2/3 cup white sugar
1-¼ teaspoons almond extract, divided
2 cups all-purpose flour
½ cup seedless raspberry jam
½ cup confectioners' sugar
1 teaspoon milk

Directions:

Preheat the oven to 350 degrees.
Cookie dough:
Beat butter and white sugar together in a medium bowl until creamy. Mix in ½ teaspoon almond extract. Add flour and mix until dough comes together.

Form dough into 1-½-inch balls and place on ungreased cookie sheets about 2 inches apart.

Use your thumb or back of measuring spoon to press down and make a dent in the center of each ball. Fill with jam.

Bake until edges are lightly browned, about 14 to 18 minutes; allow to cool on cookie sheet for a few minutes.
Drizzle:
Mix confectioners' sugar, milk, and remaining ¾ teaspoon almond extract together in a medium bowl until smooth; drizzle lightly over warm cookies.

Cranberry Walnut Pinwheel Cookies

(Submitted by Cecile VanTyne)

Ingredients:

1 cup of dried cranberries, chopped
1 cup of chopped walnuts
½ cup of sugar
Zest of one orange
2 refrigerated pie crusts
2 tablespoons of butter, melted
1 tablespoon of butter for filling
1 whole egg
2 tablespoons of water
Honey

Directions:

Preheat oven to 400 degrees.
Line a baking sheet with parchment paper and set aside.
In a pot, add cranberries, walnuts, sugar, orange zest and one tablespoon of butter until warm. Let it cool while doing the next step.
On a lightly floured surface, roll out the pie crusts into two squares.
Brush the pie crusts generously with two tablespoons of melted butter.
Spread the cooled filling onto the pie crusts. Don't overfill. Roll each pie crust into a log. Pinch the edges to seal.
Put egg and water into a small bowl and beat with a fork until combined.
Brush each log with the egg mixture.

Cut each log into ten pieces. Might want to freeze them for ten minutes to make the slicing easier.

Place on baking sheet about 1 inch apart, and bake for 12–15 minutes or until golden brown.

Let cool on a rack, then drizzle a teaspoon or more of honey on each pinwheel.

Mini Cranberry Tarts

(Submitted by Cecile VanTyne)

Ingredients:

Cinnamon sugar
1 box of puff pastry
1 cup of cranberry sauce
Butter, melted

Directions:

Preheat oven to 400 degrees and grease a cupcake pan.

If you don't already have some made, mix together some cinnamon and sugar to your liking.

Unroll puff pastry and sprinkle with the cinnamon sugar. Press gently into the dough.

Cut each puff pastry sheet into nine squares and fill each square with no more than two teaspoons of cranberry sauce. Pick up the square by the corners using your thumbs and index fingers, pinching them together as you're putting them in the cupcake pan. Sprinkle them with more cinnamon sugar.

Bake for 25–30 minutes until golden brown.

Serve cooled or warm with whipped cream or ice cream. You can also sprinkle with powdered sugar.

Recipes from Evergreen Wishes at Moonglow

❄

More Sweet Treats

Excerpt from *Evergreen Wishes at Moonglow*

Mist entered the café to find cheerful conversation and laughter flowing. A record number of cookie-exchange participants filled the room.

Betty looked the part of the ultimate holiday hostess in a soft black A-line skirt, white blouse, and red sweater vest with appliquéd snowmen and rhinestones. She'd added a reindeer antler headband to liven up the outfit as well as sparkly snowman earrings.

"We've had the most marvelous assortment of goodies today," Betty said. "Marge brought peppermint bark from the candy store, Sally made chocolate dipped orange butter cookies, Glenda showed up with peanut butter blossoms and..." Her voice trailed off as she glanced at the table, reminding herself of the extravagant spread of sugar-laden treats.

"It looks like there are brownies in the mix," Mist noted as she stepped closer to the table.

"Ginger spice brownies," Betty said. "Millie dropped those off but had to get back to the library. But look at all this." Betty pointed to other containers on the table as she circled the table. "Eggnog truffles, caramel apple cookies, butter pecan bites, and so many more!"

"The town's going to be on a sugar high until the new year," Sally said, adding a chocolate crinkle cookie to her assortment. A strand of lights flashed on and off around the base of a Santa hat she wore. "And I love these wooden trays and the fascinating wrap, Mist!"

Mist smiled. The reusable containers gave the participants something to keep. The cookies and treats were destined to disappear quickly.

Chocolate-Dipped Orange Butter Cookies

(Submitted by Diane Jewell)

Ingredients:

1 cup (2 sticks) butter, softened
1 cup confectioners' sugar
1 egg
2 ½ teaspoons pure orange extract
2 ½ cups sifted flour
¼ teaspoon salt
6 ounces semi-sweet chocolate, chopped
1 ½ teaspoons shortening

Directions:

Preheat oven to 350 degrees. Beat butter and sugar in large bowl with electric mixer on medium speed until light and fluffy. Beat in egg and 1 ½ teaspoons of the orange extract.

Gradually beat in flour and salt until well mixed. Drop dough by rounded teaspoons onto ungreased baking sheets; flatten with fork.

Bake 12 to 14 minutes or until lightly browned. Cool on baking sheets 1 minute. Remove to wire racks; cool completely.

Melt chocolate and shortening in microwavable bowl on HIGH 1 ½ minutes, stirring after 30 seconds. Add remaining 1 teaspoon extract; stir until chocolate is completely melted. Dip each cookie halfway into chocolate mixture. Let stand at room temperature or refrigerate on wax paper-lined tray 15 minutes or until chocolate is set.

Sugar Cookies

(Submitted by Rhonda Sowers)

Ingredients:

1 cup powdered sugar
1 cup sugar
1 cup corn oil
1 cup butter
1 teaspoon cream of tarter
2 eggs
1 teaspoon vanilla
4 cups + 1 tablespoon flour
1 teaspoon salt
1 teaspoon baking soda

Directions:

Cream sugars, oil, butter, and vanilla until fluffy.
Beat eggs until light and add creamed mixture.
Add flour and rest of ingredients. Blend well.
Roll into balls. Place on ungreased cookie sheet.
Press flat with glass dipped in sugar.
Bale at 375 degrees or until slightly brown.

Christmas Popcorn

(Submitted by Betty Escobar)

Ingredients:

½ cup popcorn kernels
1 bag (12 ounce) vanilla candy melts
1 ½ cups pretzels, small or broken
1 bag (10 ounces) red and green M&M's
Red and green holiday sprinkles

Directions:

Pop the popcorn and discard unpopped kernels. Add pretzels and M&M's.

Melt the candy melts in a microwave-safe bowl for 30 seconds at 50% power. Stir and repeat until melted and smooth.

Pour half the melted candy over the popcorn/pretzel mixture and stir.

Drizzle remaining melted candy over the mixture. Do not over stir.

Pour mixture onto wax paper and add sprinkles. Allow to cool.

Break into pieces and store in an airtight container.

Chocolate Candy Cane Fudge

(Submitted by Rhonda Gothier)

Ingredients:

1 bag chocolate chips
1 can condensed milk
Candy canes

Directions:

Melt 1 bag chocolate chips. Add can condensed milk.
Pour in greased foil-lined 9 x 9 pan.
Crush a few candy canes and sprinkle on top.
Refrigerate until solid.
Pull out of pan using foil liner and cut in squares.
Store in airtight container.

Ice Box Fruitcake

(Submitted by Alma Collins)

Ingredients:

1 ½ cups butter
1 lb. chopped dates
16 oz. small marshmallows
1 lb. vanilla wafers, crushed
2 teaspoons vanilla
4 tablespoons brown sugar
1 lb. candied fruit
4 cups pecans, chopped
2 pkg. coconut

Directions:

Over low heat, melt the butter, dates, and marshmallows. Mix the rest of the ingredients except the coconut in a large bowl.

When the butter, dates, and marshmallow mixture is melted, pour over the other ingredients and mix well.

Pour 1 pkg. coconut on waxed paper. Roll fruitcake into logs (whatever size you prefer) then roll logs in coconut to cover.

Wrap each log in aluminum foil and refrigerate until set. Slice each log into slices.

Dayna's Oatmeal Cookies

(Submitted by Dayna Crandall)

Ingredients:

1 cup shortening
¾ cup brown sugar
¾ cup sugar
1 teaspoon vanilla
2 eggs
½ teaspoon water
1 ⅓ cups flour
2 cups rolled oats
1 teaspoon baking soda
1 teaspoon salt
2 teaspoons cinnamon
2 cups walnuts (optional)
1 large pkg. semisweet chocolate chips (optional)

Directions:

Cream sugar and shortening. Beat in vanilla, eggs, and water.
Combine dry ingredients and stir in.
Fold in chips and nuts if desired.
Press balls flat or drop 1 tablespoon-sized onto ungreased baking sheet.
Bake at 375 degrees for 10-12 minutes.

Date Nut Torte Squares

(Submitted by Molly Elliott)

Ingredients:

1 cup chopped dates
1 cup chopped nuts
1 cup sugar
2 eggs, beaten
2 tablespoons flour
1 teaspoon baking powder

Directions:

Mix all ingredients together and bake at 300 degrees for 30 minutes.

Cut into squares and dust with powdered sugar.

Salted Peanut Cookies

(Submitted by Brenda Ellis)

Ingredients:

1 cup shortening
2 cup brown sugar
2 eggs, beaten
2 cups flour
1 teaspoon baking soda
1 teaspoon baking powder
½ teaspoon salt
2 cups oatmeal
1 cup Wheaties
1 cup chopped, salted peanuts

Directions:

Cream shortening and sugar. Blend in eggs.
Add sifted dry ingredients.
Add oatmeal, Wheaties, and peanuts.
Drop by teaspoon and flatten with a fork dipped in sugar.
Bake at 350 degrees for approximately 12 minutes or until done.

Cranberry White Chocolate Bars

(Submitted by Molly Elliott)

Ingredients:

2 large eggs
½ teaspoon vanilla extract
1 cup sugar
1 cup all-purpose flour
¼ teaspoon salt
½ cup butter, melted
¾ cups fresh or frozen (thawed) cranberries, coarsely chopped
½ (11-oz) bag white chocolate chips

Directions:

Preheat oven to 350 degrees.
Whisk together eggs and vanilla extract in a mixing bowl until blended. Gradually add sugar, beating until blended.
Stir in flour, salt, and melted butter.
Gently stir in cranberries and white chocolate chips.
Spread dough in a lightly greased 8-inch square pan.
Bake 38 to 40 minutes or until a toothpick inserted in center comes out clean.
Cool and cut into bars.

Caramel Apple Cookies

(Submitted by Shelia Hall)

Ingredients:

Cookies:
½ cup shortening
1 ¼ cups packed brown sugar
1 egg
½ cup apple juice
2 ¼ cups whole wheat pastry flour or all-purpose flour
1 teaspoon baking soda
1 teaspoon ground cinnamon
¼ teaspoon ground cloves
¼ teaspoon salt
1 medium tart apple, peeled, cored, and coarsely shredded (1 cup)
¾ cup golden raisins

Frosting:
2 tablespoon margarine
⅓ cup packed light brown sugar
2 tablespoons water
1 ¾ cups sifted powdered sugar
Fat-free milk
⅓ cup finely chopped walnuts

Directions:

Preheat oven to 350 degrees. Beat shortening and add the 1 ¼ cups brown sugar with an electric mixer on medium speed until combined. Add egg; beat 1 minute. Add apple juice; beat at low speed until blended. Stir together flour, baking soda, cinnamon, cloves, and salt. Add to egg mixture, beating at low speed until combined. Fold in apple and raisins.

Drop dough by slightly rounded teaspoonfuls 1-½ inches apart onto ungreased cookie sheet. Bake in preheated oven for 8 minutes or until edges are lightly browned. Let stand 1 minute on cookie sheet. Remove to wire racks and cool.

For the frosting, heat margarine, ⅓ cup brown sugar, and water over medium-high heat, stirring until sugar dissolves. Remove from heat. Stir in sifted powdered sugar. If frosting begins to harden, stir in small amount of fat-free milk to make a spreading consistency. Spread cookies with caramel frosting and sprinkle with walnuts. Makes about 72.

Gluten-Free Chocolate Chip Cookies

(submitted by Petrenia Etheridge)

Ingredients:

2 bananas, mashed
1 cup oats
½ cup choc chips
1 teaspoon cinnamon
1 teaspoon vanilla

Directions:

Mix ingredients together and spoon onto parchment paper. Bake at 350 degrees for 20 min.

Pecan Cheese Wafers

(Submitted by Petrenia Etheridge)

Ingredients:

1 cup shredded cheese
1 stick butter
½ cup all-purpose flour
1 cup chopped pecans
1 teaspoon seasoning of choice

Directions:

Cream butter and cheese. Mix seasoning in flour then add to mixture.
Continue mixing as you add in pecans.
Roll into small balls and smash flat.
Bake at 350 degrees for 10-12 minutes.

Gingerbread Kiss Cookies

(Submitted by Kim Davis of Cinnamon and Sugar and a Little Bit of Murder blog)

Ingredients:

¾ cup unsalted butter, room temperature
¾ cup brown sugar, packed
½ cup molasses
1 egg, room temperature
1 teaspoon vanilla extract
3 cups all-purpose flour
2 teaspoon ground ginger
1 teaspoon ground cinnamon
½ teaspoon ground nutmeg
½ teaspoon allspice
1 teaspoon salt
1 teaspoon baking soda
Coarse sparkling sugar (regular granulated sugar can be substituted)
1 bag chocolate striped Hershey Kisses (regular Hershey Kisses can be substituted), unwrapped

Directions:

In a large bowl, whisk together the flour, ginger, cinnamon, nutmeg, allspice, baking soda, and salt. Set aside.

In the bowl of a stand mixer, beat the brown sugar and butter together until light and fluffy. Add in the molasses, egg, and vanilla extract and beat until well combined.

Slowly add the dry ingredients and mix until incorporated.

Cover with plastic wrap and refrigerate the dough for 30 to 60 minutes.

Preheat oven to 350 degrees and line 2 baking sheets with parchment paper.

Form the chilled dough into small walnut-sized balls. Roll each ball in the coarse sparkling sugar then place on the prepared baking sheets.

Bake for 8 to 10 minutes.

Remove from the oven and place a Hershey Kiss into the center of the cookies. Cool on the baking sheet for 5 minutes then remove to a wire rack to cool completely before serving. Makes 40–45 cookies depending on size.

Million-Dollar Fudge

(Submitted by Sally Jo Walker)

Ingredients:

12 ounces semisweet chocolate morsels
12 ounces sweet chocolate, broken into small pieces
2 cups marshmallow cream
4 ½ cups sugar
Pinch salt
2 tablespoons butter
1 ½ cups (12 ounces) canned evaporated milk
2 cups coarsely chopped nuts (optional)

Directions:

Stir together all chocolate and marshmallow cream.
Bring sugar, salt, butter, and evaporated milk to a boil. Lower heat and simmer 7 minutes.
Pour the hot mixture over the chocolate and marshmallow cream and mix.
Stir in the chopped nuts.
Pour into a greased 9x13 baking dish. Let stand until firm.

Almond Crunch Bars

(Submitted by Betty Escobar)

Ingredients:

1 ½ cups chocolate chips
½ cup almond butter
¼ teaspoon salt
2 cups rice cereal

Directions:

Melt chocolate chips, almond butter, and salt together, stirring until smooth.

Place rice cereal in a bowl and pour the melted mixture over it. Stir until evenly coated.

Place parchment paper into a greased 9x5 loaf pan. The greased pan will hold the parchment paper in place.

Press the mixture into the loaf pan and smooth the top.

Set in the freezer for 1 hour to firm up.

Lift out with parchment paper and cut into 1-inch bars.

Keep in an airtight container in the fridge for 2 weeks or freeze for up to 3 months.

Pecan Fingers

(Submitted by Shelia Hall)

Ingredients:

6 tablespoons butter
3oz. shortening
¾ cup confectioners' sugar
1 ½ cups plain flour
2 eggs
1 cup packed brown sugar
2 tablespoons flour
½ teaspoon baking powder
½ teaspoon salt
½ teaspoon vanilla
1 cup pecans

Directions:

Heat oven to 350 degrees.
Cream together shortening, butter, and confectioners' sugar. Blend in flour.
Press evenly in bottom of a 13x9 ungreased baking pan.
Bake 12-15 minutes. Mix remaining ingredients and spread over hot baked layer.
Return to oven and bake 20 minutes.
Let cool then cut into 3x1-inch bars.

Momma's Sour Cream Walnuts

(Submitted by Lanette Fields)

Ingredients:

½ cup of sour cream
1 cup packed dark brown sugar
½ cup granulated sugar
1 teaspoon real vanilla
2 ½ cups of walnut halves

Directions:

Cook first 3 ingredients over medium heat until candy thermometer reaches 236 degrees.
Remove from heat and add vanilla. Beat until mixture starts to thicken.
Add walnuts and stir until well coated.
Turn out onto greased or parchment-lined cookie sheet. Break into pieces.

Red Velvet Cake Cookies

(Submitted by Colleen Galster)

Ingredients:

1 box of Red Velvet Cake Mix, any brand
2 large eggs
½ cup unsalted butter, melted
1-½ cups of your mix in (white chocolate chips are my favorite) or skip this if desired
Cream cheese frosting (if desired) or sprinkles/toppings of choice

Suggestions to mix in:
White Chocolate Chips
Chocolate Chips
Butterscotch Chips
Caramel
Sprinkles
M&M's
Petite Mints

Directions:

Place cake mix, eggs, and butter in a large bowl. Stir until the batter is smooth. You can do this with a wooden spoon or a hand mixer. Stir in add-ins of your choice, if using.
Scoop 2 tablespoon sized cookie dough balls onto cookie sheets lined with parchment paper. Chill for at least one hour.
Preheat oven to 350 degrees. Bake chilled cookies for about 11-13 minutes, or until the edges just start to get golden brown.

If desired, frost cooled cookies with cream cheese frosting.

Store in an airtight container for up to 3 days or freeze for up to one month.

Cheesecake Stuffed Strawberry Cookies

(Submitted by Nettie Moore from the blog Moore or Less Cooking)

Ingredients:

15 oz strawberry cake mix
⅓ cup of oil
1 teaspoon of vanilla
2 eggs
1 cup of white chocolate chips
1 (8 oz) block of cream cheese
1 teaspoon vanilla
3 tablespoons sugar

Directions:

In a large bowl mix cake mix, oil, vanilla, and eggs and mix with a hand mixer until nice and smooth. Add in white chocolate chips and mix again.
Place bowl in the fridge for 20 minutes.
In a medium-large bowl mix cream cheese, sugar, and vanilla. Mix with a hand mixer until smooth.
Place parchment paper on a tray. Using an ice cream scooper, scoop balls and drop them onto the paper, it should make 12. Place in the freezer for 40 minutes or until the cookie mixture is done.
Place parchment paper down on a large baking sheet. Roll 1 ½ inch amounts of cookie mixture into balls.
Once all 12 are laid out on paper, place them inside the fridge again for 40 minutes.
Preheat oven to 350 degrees while waiting. Flatten the

cookie mixture out, and place 1 cream cheese ball inside it. Roll into a ball using your hands, making sure the cream cheese doesn't leak out.

Once all rolled out, place into the preheated oven for 10-12 minutes.

When done, set out to cool and enjoy!

Tips:

If the cookie mixture is too sticky when handling, place it in the fridge for 20 more minutes.

Add more chocolate chips to the outside of the dough balls before placing them into the oven.

Make sure you can't see any cream cheese when you roll it into a ball so it doesn't leak out.

Graham Cracker Toffee Bars

(Submitted by Nettie Moore from the blog Moore or Less Cooking)

Ingredients:

12 graham crackers, broken in half (24 squares in total)
1 stick of butter
¾ cup of brown sugar
6 ounces semisweet chocolate chips
1 cup chopped pecans

Directions:

Gather all the ingredients. Pre-heat your oven to 350 degrees.

Get a 12x18 sheet pan and line it with foil and spray with non-stick spray.

Arrange graham crackers in a square. (Make sure they are touching.)

In a saucepan, bring butter and brown sugar to a boil on medium heat. Cook for two minutes while stirring constantly until melted and bubbly.

Immediately pour over graham crackers and spread evenly.

Bake in the oven for approximately 6 minutes, until light brown and bubbly.

Sprinkle chocolate chips all over the crackers, then bake again for 2 minutes.

Take out of the oven and spread the chocolate chips over the crackers.

Sprinkle with pecans. Lightly press the pecans down into the chocolate.

Cool completely and break into squares.

Tips and Tricks:

Instead of pecans, use pretzels or peanuts.
Add extra chocolate chips if you like it a little more on the chocolate side.
You can use dark chocolate instead of milk chocolate!

Wassail

(Submitted by Elizabeth Christy with gratitude to Patricia Christy)

Ingredients:

2 quarts apple cider
½ cup sugar
¼ cup firmly packed brown sugar
2 cinnamon sticks
12 whole cloves
4 cups of grapefruit juice
4 cups of orange juice
1 cup of pineapple juice

Directions:

Combine the apple cider, sugar, brown sugar, cinnamon sticks, and cloves and bring to a boil.
Cook until the sugar dissolves. Reduce heat and simmer for 5 minutes.
Add the grapefruit, orange, and pineapple juices.
Heat until hot, but do not boil. Strain out the chunks.
May be refrigerated and reheated as needed or wanted.

Recipes from Angels at Moonglow

More Sweet Treats

Excerpt from *Angels at Moonglow*

Mist took care as she stepped from the house just past five a.m. The chilly wind and icy sidewalk led her to tread carefully as she walked the half block that separated home from work. Arriving at the hotel, she quietly let herself in.

She relished these quiet hours when she could prepare fresh-baked goods and have time to think. Being alone at the beginning of the day helped her put the day in order—what tasks needed attending, what food would be prepared, which guests would be arriving, and what the likely timing of all of it would be. As she fixed herself a cup of tea and began to mix ingredients for cranberry scones, she reviewed plans for the rest of the day. In this case, it involved serving a simple breakfast in the café, then greeting the guest arrivals, then hopefully a trip to Duffy's to see how the angel ornament project was going, and then offering another meal in the cafe that evening. It would be a busy day but fulfilling, which made it all worthwhile.

Everything she did for the hotel or town felt like a blessing, more for herself than for anyone else, though many would argue with that. There were times when she wondered how she could possibly have ended up so lucky. She'd found the perfect town, the perfect job, the perfect partner, and certainly the perfect miniature of herself, which is how close friends described Rain. She could create art, could delight in preparing culinary feasts, could breathe in the clean mountain air, and could bask in the peaceful town ambiance. It was a perfect life in so many ways, and she was eternally grateful for it.

Snowball Cookies

(Submitted by Shelia Hall)

Ingredients:

1 cup unsalted butter softened
5 tablespoons granulated sugar
2 teaspoons pure vanilla extract
1/4 teaspoon fine-grain sea salt
2 cups all-purpose flour
2 cups finely chopped walnuts, almonds or pecans
1 1/2 cups confectioners sugar

Directions:

Blend softened butter with powdered sugar. Add vanilla. Mix in salt, flour, and chopped pecans.

Form dough into 1-inch balls or flattened cookies and place on an ungreased cookie sheet.

Bake at 325 degrees for 20 minutes. Roll in powdered sugar while hot. Let cool and roll again in powdered sugar.

Frosted Gingerbread Cookies

(Submitted by Petrenia Etheridge)

Ingredients:

1/2 cup butter
1/2 cup brown sugar, packed
1/2 cup molasses
1 teaspoon salt
2 teaspoons cinnamon
2 teaspoons ginger
1 teaspoon vanilla
1 egg
2-3 cups self rising flour

Frosting:
1-2 cups powdered sugar
1 teaspoon vanilla
2 tablespoons milk

Directions:

In a saucepan, melt butter and stir in sugar, salt, and molasses. Add in cinnamon and ginger and stir well.
Remove from heat and add vanilla and egg and stir well.
Slowly pour into 2 cups flour and mix. Add in extra flour as needed for rolled cookies.
Roll into a ball and cover with plastic wrap and chill for 1-2 hrs.
Roll out onto floured surface about 1/4 inch thick and use gingerbread man cookie cutter or round biscuit cutter.

Bake at 350 degrees for 8-10 minutes. Frost when completely cool.

Josie's Fudge

(Submitted by Catherine Ann Tremble)

Ingredients:

3 cups of sugar
2/3 cups of evaporated milk
1 1/2 sticks of butter
1 package chocolate chips
1 jar marshmallow cream
1 teaspoon vanilla

Directions:

Put sugar, evaporated milk, and butter in medium size pan and cook over medium high heat, stirring constantly until a rolling boil. Cook for 5 minutes.
Remove from heat, and add one package of chocolate chips. Stir until mixed well.
Add a jar of marshmallow cream. Mix well. Add vanilla extract. Stir well.
Drop by tablespoons onto foil to create "fudge drops."
Option: Pour half of the mixture into a bread pan. Top with coconut/condensed milk mixture, then top that with the rest of the fudge to make a "mounds" fudge.

Crème Brûlée Cookies

(Submitted by Petrenia Etheridge)

Ingredients:

1/2 cup butter, softened
1/2 cup oil
1/2 cup sugar
1/2 cup powdered sugar
1 large egg
2 teaspoon vanilla
2 cups all purpose flour
1/2 teaspoon baking soda
1/2 teaspoon salt

Frosting
Block of cream cheese, softened
6 tablespoons butter, softened
2 1/2 cups powdered sugar
1/2 teaspoon granulated sugar per cookie

Directions:

Mix butter, oil, and sugars and beat on high for about 4 minutes.
Add egg and vanilla and beat until combined.
Mix dry ingredients and add to mixture at low speed until combined.
Use ice-cream scoop or spoon and scoop about 2 tbsp dough and form into balls and flatten halfway on a cookie sheet with parchment paper. Cover and chill for 2-3 hrs.

More Sweet Treats

Bake at 350 degrees for 8 minutes. Let cool on cookie sheet.

For frosting, mix butter and cream cheese until fluffy. Add powdered sugar. Spread on cookies and sprinkle granulated sugar on top. Option: Use a torch to brûlée the tops.

Easy Christmas Bark

(Submitted by Lanette Fields)

Ingredients:

10-12 oz package of butterscotch chips
10-12 oz package of white chocolate chips
10-12 oz package of milk chocolate chips
10-12 oz package of dark chocolate chips
10-12 oz package of semisweet chocolate chips
9.5-10 oz package of mini milk chocolate M&Ms
16 oz can of cocktail peanuts (use 1/2 can or to taste)

Directions:

Line 2 large baking sheets including sides with parchment paper. Set aside.

Add all baking chips together in a microwave-safe bowl and heat 3 minutes at a time. Stir melted mixture until smooth.

Add half a can of peanuts and all M&Ms and stir until well mixed.

Quickly pour mixture evenly onto each baking sheet and smooth out.

Chill in refrigerator until set.

Break into pieces. If too hard to break apart, set out for 30 minutes.

Serve immediately or store in freezer-safe container for up to 3 months.

Orange Crisps

(Submitted by Brenda Ellis)

Ingredients:

1 cup shortening
1 teaspoon grated orange peel
1/2 cup sugar
2 1/2 cups flour
1/2 cup brown sugar
1/4 teaspoon salt
1 tablespoon orange juice
1/4 teaspoon baking soda
1 egg

Directions:

Cream shortening. Add sugar and orange juice and cream well. Add egg and orange peel.
Sift flour, salt, and soda together, adding a little at a time to the shortening mixture.
Place by teaspoon full on an ungreased cookie sheet.
Bake at 375 degrees for 10 to 12 minutes.
Yields 7 dozen small cookies.
Option: Can substitute lemon in place of orange.

Gingerbread Sandwich Cookies

(Submitted by Cecile VanTyne)

Ingredients:

Cookie Ingredients:
2 cups of all-purpose flour
2 teaspoon ground cinnamon
1/2 teaspoon ground ginger
½ teaspoon nutmeg
½ teaspoon salt
1/4 teaspoon ground cloves
3/4 teaspoon baking soda
3/4 cup packed light brown sugar
8 tablespoons unsalted butter, melted
1/4 cup molasses
3 tablespoons crystallized ginger, finally chopped (no substitution)
1 large egg
1/4 cup buttermilk
1 teaspoon vanilla extract

Cream Cheese Filling:
6 tablespoons unsalted butter, room temperature
1 1/2 cups powdered sugar
6 oz cream cheese cut into 6-8 pieces, softened
1/2 teaspoon vanilla extract
Pinch of salt

Garnish
Powdered sugar for dusting

Directions:

Whisk flour, cinnamon, ground ginger, nutmeg, salt, cloves, and baking soda together in a medium bowl. Set aside.

Whisk brown sugar, melted butter, molasses, and crystallized ginger in a separate large bowl until combined. Whisk in egg, buttermilk and vanilla until combined. Add flour mixture and stir with a rubber spatula just until the dough comes together. Cover bowl with plastic wrap and refrigerate for at least 1 hour up to 24.

Preheat oven to 350 degrees. Line two baking sheets with parchment paper or a nonstick mat. Roll dough into balls using one scant tablespoon. Space balls evenly about 2 inches apart. Bake cookies one sheet at a time, until puffed and just set about 11-13 minutes. Let cookies cool on sheet for 5 minutes then transfer to wire rack to cool completely before frosting.

Using a stand mixer fitted w/paddle attachment, beat butter and powdered sugar on med-high speed until fluffy, about 2 minutes. With mixer running, add cream cheese 1 piece at a time and continue to beat until smooth, about 30 seconds. Beat in vanilla extract and a pinch of salt as needed.

Spoon or pipe 1 tablespoon of frosting evenly onto the bottom of 24 cookies. Top with remaining 24 cookies, bottom sides down. (If the frosting is very soft, refrigerate for 15 minutes before filling.) Then dust with powdered sugar.

Store cookies in an airtight container in the fridge. Bring to room temp before serving. Enjoy!

The Best Old-Fashioned Molasses Sugar Cookies

(Submitted by Alma Collins)

Ingredients:

1-1/2 cups butter, softened
2 cups granulated sugar
½ cup dark molasses
2 eggs, beaten
4 teaspoons baking soda
4 cups all-purpose flour
1 teaspoon ground cloves (I used allspice)
1 teaspoon ground ginger
2 teaspoons ground cinnamon
1 teaspoon salt
Turbinado or sparkling sugar to coat the unbaked cookies

Directions:

In a medium bowl, beat the sugar and butter until light and fluffy. Stir in the eggs and molasses until completely blended.

In a separate large bowl, mix all the remaining dry ingredients together.

Add the butter mixture to the flour mixture and mix until combined completely.

Cover the dough tightly and refrigerate overnight.

IMPORTANT: The dough needs to be thoroughly chilled. Allow at least 4-6 hours to chill. When the dough is ready to be rolled, it will be very stiff.

Preheat the oven to 350 degrees.

Roll the dough into 1-inch balls and coat them with the Turbinado sugar.

More Sweet Treats

Bake the cookies on a sheet pan, placed 1-2 inches apart, for 10-12 minutes. The cookies should crackle on top and have golden edges. Recipe makes 6-8 dozen, depending on size.

Crackle Double Chocolate Cookies

(Submitted by Patti Rusk)

Ingredients:

1 box of chocolate cake mix
1 1/2 cups chocolate chips
1 8oz tub Cool Whip
1 egg
1 1/2 cups powdered sugar
Spray oil for cookie scoop or hands

Directions:

Using whisk, mix cake mix (dry from box), egg, and Cool Whip until well blended. Stir in chocolate chips.

Using sprayed cookie scoop or sprayed hands, form into 1-inch round balls. Roll in powdered sugar.

Bake at 350 degrees for 12-15 minutes. Cool completely in wire rack.

Store in airtight container.

Walnut Butter Cookies

(Submitted by Patti Rusk)

Ingredients:

1 cup salted butter, softened
2 cups powder sugar
1 3/4 cups all-purpose flour
1 cup chopped walnuts
1 teaspoon vanilla extract

Directions:

In a large mixing bowl, combine butter and 1 cup powder sugar. With electric mixer, beat at medium speed until light and creamy.

Add flour, walnuts, and vanilla extract, continue beating until blended.

Divide dough in half and roll each half into an 8-inch log. Wrap logs in plastic wrap and refrigerate overnight.

Slice logs into 1/2-inch slices. Placing 2 inches apart on parchment-lined baking sheet. Freeze for 15 minutes.

Bake at 350 degrees for 12 minutes until edges of cookies are golden brown. Cool completely on wire rack.

In shallow dish, dredge cookies with remaining 1 cup of powder sugar.

Serve immediately or store in airtight container separated by wax paper.

Glazed Fruitcake Cookies

(Submitted by Patti Rusk)

Ingredients:

1 1/4 cups spiced rum
1/2 cup finely chopped candied red cherries
1/2 cup finely chopped candied green cherries
1/2 cup finely chopped dried pineapple
1/2 cup finely chopped crystallized ginger
1/2 cup finely chopped candied orange
1 cup unsalted butter, softened (not melted)
1 3/4 cups sugar divided
1/4 cup light brown sugar firmly packed
2 large eggs, room temperature
1 teaspoon rum extract
3 1/2 cups all purpose flour
1 teaspoon baking soda
1 teaspoon salt
1 teaspoon nutmeg
1 teaspoon ground cinnamon
1 teaspoon round ginger
1/2 teaspoon ground cloves
1 cup chopped toasted pecans

Directions:

In medium microwave-safe bowl, combined rum, cherries, pineapple, crystallized ginger, and orange, microwave on high until hot 2-3 minutes. Let stand at room temperature for at least one hour stirring occasionally. Drain fruit mixture. Set aside.

More Sweet Treats

Preheat oven to 350 degrees.

Using a stand mixer fitted with a paddle, beat the butter, 1 1/4 cups of gradated sugar and brown sugar at medium speed until fluffy, 2-3 minutes, occasionally scrape the size of the bowl. The eggs, one at a time beating well after each addition. Beat in rum extract.

In a medium bowl, whisk together flour, baking soda, salt, nutmeg, cinnamon, ground ginger, and cloves. Add flour mixture to butter mixture all at once. Beat at low speed just until combined stopping to scrape sides of bowl. Fold in the fruit mixture and pecans. Dough will be sticky.

On a rimmed plate, place remaining 1/2 cup of granulated sugar. Using a 2 tbsp cookie scoop, scoop dough and shape into balls. Roll in sugar and place 1 1/2-2 inches apart on baking sheets lined with parchment paper. Using the palm of your hand, gently flatten the balls into 1-inch thickness.

Bake until light gold brown and cookies are set around edges about 12 minutes. Let cool for three minutes on baking sheets and let cool completely on wire racks.

Place Rum Drizzle in a pastry bag and drizzle onto cooled cookies.

Rum Drizzle
1 cup powder sugar
1 1/2 tablespoons heavy whipping cream
1 tablespoon spiced rum
2 teaspoon unsalted butter melted
1/4 teaspoon salt

In medium bowl stir together all ingredients until smooth. Use immediately.

Dutch Letter Almond Bars

(Submitted by Vera Kenyon)

Ingredients:

1 cup butter, melted
1 - 7 or 8 oz package of almond paste
2 eggs plus 1 egg yolk, (save the egg white)
1 1/2 cups sugar
2 cups flour- white or almond
2 teaspoons of almond extract
1/2 teaspoon vanilla
Sliced almonds
Coarse sugar like Turbinado or a colored sugar

Directions:

Preheat the oven to 325 degrees.
In mixer, combine ingredients and blend well.
Spread into a 9x13 or 10x15 inch pan. Brush with whipped egg white.
Sprinkle with sliced almonds and sugar.
Bake for 25-30 minutes until golden brown. Be careful not to overbake.

Red Velvet Cupcakes

(Submitted by Alisha Collins)

Ingredients:

2 1/2 cups flour
1/2 cup unsweetened cocoa powder
1 teaspoon baking soda
1/2 teaspoon salt
2 cups sugar
1 cup (2 sticks) butter, at room temperature
4 eggs at room temperature
1 cup sour cream
1/2 cup buttermilk
1 bottle (1 ounce) red food coloring
2 teaspoons vanilla extract

Directions:

Preheat oven to 350 degrees and line 30 cupcake cups.
In a separate bowl, whisk together the flour, cocoa, baking soda, and salt. Set aside.
Cream together the butter and sugar together on medium speed until light and fluffy. This usually takes about 5 minutes.
Beat in eggs one at a time until fully incorporated, scraping bowl down between each egg.
Mix in sour cream, buttermilk, food coloring, and vanilla.
Gradually mix in flour mixture until just combined. Don't overmix!
Spoon batter into muffin cups until 2/3 full.
Bake 20-25 minutes until toothpick comes out clean.

Cool in pans for 5 minutes and then turn out onto wire racks to cool completely.

Tips:
   *If you don't have buttermilk, you can mix 1 tablespoon of vinegar or lemon juice to enough sweet milk (regular milk) to make 1 cup. Mix together and allow to set 5 minutes before using in recipe. If you only need 1/2 cup cut measurements in half.
   *Adjust cooking time by 10-15 minutes if making a multiple layer cake instead of cupcakes.
   *For a deeper chocolate flavor, use a dark cocoa and add 1 tablespoon more than what the recipe calls for.

Frosting:
   Vanilla Cream Cheese Frosting

   1 8 ounce package of cream cheese, softened
   1/4 cup (1/2 stick) butter, softened
   2 tablespoons sour cream
   2 teaspoons vanilla
   1 16 ounce package confectioner's sugar (10X), approximately 3 1/2 cups

   Cream together the cream cheese, butter, sour cream, and vanilla on medium speed until light and fluffy (approximately 3-4 minutes).
   Gradually blend in the powdered sugar until smooth and spreadable.
   Spread on cupcakes or your layer cake and enjoy.

Sour Cream Sugar Cookies

(Submitted by Betty Rufledt)

Ingredients:

2 cups sugar
3 eggs
1 cup sour cream
1 teaspoon soda
1 1/4 cups shortening
2 teaspoons vanilla
1 teaspoon baking powder
5 cups flour

Directions:

Cream sugar, shortening and eggs until fluffy. Add vanilla and sour cream.
Gradually add dry ingredients.
Refrigerate for 1 1/2 hrs. Roll 1/4 of dough.
Roll out 1/2 inch for thick cookies or thinner if desired.
Cut into shapes and sprinkle with sugar and place on greased cookie sheet.
Bake at 375 for 10 minutes until set.

Rolo Cookie Bars (Gluten-Free Version)

(Submitted by Colleen Galster)

Ingredients:

3/4 cup butter
3/4 cup brown sugar
1 teaspoon vanilla extract
1 large egg
1 egg yolk
1 3/4 cups gluten free flour
1/2 teaspoon baking soda
1/4 teaspoon salt
1 cup chocolate chips
1 1/2 cups Rolo candies

Directions:

Preheat oven to 350 degrees. Grease and line an 8-inch square pan with parchment paper making sure the 2 sides overhang.
In a large mixing bowl cream butter and brown sugar until pale and creamy. Add vanilla, egg and the egg yolk and beat with mixer until combined.
Add flour, baking soda and salt and beat until a soft dough forms.
Add chocolate chips and mix well. Divide the dough in half and press the first half into the bottom of the pan to form an even layer. Scatter Rolo candies all over the dough.
Take the other half of the dough and break it into pieces and place it on top of the Rolos. Gently spread it out so most of the Rolos are covered.

Cook for approximately 18-20 minutes or until golden brown. Leave to cool completely in the pan. Cut into bars and enjoy!

Sparkling Angel Cookies

(Submitted by Kim Davis of Cinnamon and Sugar and a Little Bit of Murder)

Using a boxed cake mix for the base, these light, chewy cookies are a breeze to make.

Makes 3 dozen

Ingredients:

1 box Angel Food cake mix
1 egg
1/3 cup water
1/2 teaspoon orange extract
Coarse sparkling sugar, or your color choice of sanding sugar.

Directions:

Line a baking sheet with parchment paper. This is a must as the cookies are sticky!

Add the cake mix to a large bowl. Whisk the egg, water, and extract together, then stir into the cake mix until smooth. Dough will be loose. Chill for 1 hour.

Preheat the oven to 350 degrees.

Using a tablespoon-sized cookie scoop, drop spoonfuls of dough onto the prepared baking sheet. Space them at least 2 to 3 inches apart since these cookies spread.

Generously sprinkle the tops of the unbaked cookies with sparkling sugar (or your choice of sanding sugar).

Bake for 9 to 10 minutes until edges are a light golden color. Remove from oven and cool cookies on the baking sheet for 10 minutes, then transfer to a wire rack to cool completely.

Store leftovers in an airtight container with parchment or wax paper between the layers.

Pecan Kisses

(Submitted by Petrenia Etheridge)

Ingredients:

1 egg white, beaten stiff
1/2 cup brown sugar
1 teaspoon vanilla
2- 2 1/2 cups pecan halves

Directions:

Mix together stiff egg white, sugar and vanilla.

Dip pecan halves in mixture to cover completely and place individually on a greased baking sheet or parchment paper about 2 inches apart.

Bake at 200 for 30 minutes, turn oven off and leave pecans in for another 30 minutes. Take out and place in candy dish.

Old-Fashioned Sugar Cookies

Recipe from the 1800s
   (Submitted by Betty Escobar)

   Ingredients:
   1 cup (two sticks) butter, softened
   1 cup sugar
   2 eggs, beaten well
   1 tablespoon milk
   2 teaspoons vanilla
   2-3 cups flour
   1 teaspoon baking powder

   Directions:

   Cream butter and sugar together. Sift baking powder with flour.
   Add milk, well beaten eggs, and vanilla.
   Add enough flour to roll out. Cut into desired shapes with cookie cutters.
   Bake at 375 degrees for ten minutes.
   Tip: This is a typical Victorian recipe, which was simply a list of ingredients and essentially no instructions. Recommend starting with 2 cups of flour and then adding more as needed to get the dough to a consistency where you are able to pinch the dough together and form a ball.

Iced Peppermint Candy Cookies

(Submitted by Molly Elliott)

Ingredients:

1/2 cup butter (one stick), softened
1/3 cup white sugar
1 large egg, beaten
1 1/2 cups all-purpose flour
1/8 teaspoon salt
2 tablespoons water
1 teaspoon vanilla
1/4 cup crushed peppermint candy canes
Option: Use toffee bits instead of crushed candy canes

Icing:
1/3 cup confectioners' sugar
3 teaspoons warm water
1 tablespoon crushed peppermint candy canes, or to taste

Directions:

Cream butter and sugar together. Add egg.
Add flour and salt. Mix all ingredients together.
Add crushed candy canes and form combine to form a soft dough.
Roll into balls the size of a small walnut and place 1 inch apart on greased cookie sheets.
Bake at 350 degrees for 10-12 minutes. Let cool a few minutes on cookie sheet before moving to a wire rack.

Icing:

Mix powdered sugar and water together until smooth.

Dip cooled cookies into the icing and then sprinkle with crushed candy canes. Let set before serving.

Recipe Notes

Recipe Notes

Books by Deborah Garner

The Paige MacKenzie Series

Above the Bridge

When NY reporter Paige MacKenzie arrives in Jackson Hole, it's not long before her instincts tell her there's more than a basic story to be found in the popular, northwestern Wyoming mountain area. A chance encounter with attractive cowboy Jake Norris soon has Paige chasing a legend of buried treasure passed down through generations. Sidestepping a few shady characters who are also searching for the same hidden reward, she will have to decide who is trustworthy and who is not.

The Moonglow Café

The discovery of an old diary inside the wall of the historic hotel soon sends NY reporter Paige MacKenzie into the underworld of art and deception. Each of the town's residents holds a key to untangling more than one long-buried secret, from the hippie chick owner of a new age café to the mute homeless man in the town park. As the worlds of Western art and sapphire mining collide, Paige finds herself juggling research, romance, and danger.

Three Silver Doves

The New Mexico resort of Agua Encantada seems a perfect destination for reporter Paige MacKenzie to combine work with well-deserved rest and relaxation. But when suspicious jewelry shows up on another guest, and the town's storyteller goes missing, Paige's R&R is soon redefined as restlessness and risk. Will an unexpected overnight trip to Tierra Roja Casino lead her to the answers she seeks, or are darker secrets lurking along the way?

Hutchins Creek Cache

When a mysterious 1920s coin is discovered behind the Hutchins Creek Railroad Museum in Colorado, Paige MacKenzie starts digging into four generations of Hutchins family history, with a little help from the Denver Mint. As legends of steam engines and coin mintage mingle, will Paige discover the true origin of the coin, or will she find herself riding the rails dangerously close to more than one long-hidden town secret?

Crazy Fox Ranch

As Paige MacKenzie returns to Jackson Hole, she has only two things on her mind: enjoy life with Wyoming's breathtaking Grand Tetons as the backdrop and spend more time with handsome cowboy Jake Norris as he prepares to open his guest ranch. But when a stranger's odd behavior leads her to research Western filming in the area—in particular, the movie *Shane*, will it simply lead to a freelance article for the *Manhattan Post*, or will it lead to a dangerous, hidden secret?

Sweet Sierra Gulch

Paige MacKenzie isn't convinced there's anything "sweet" about Sweet Sierra Gulch when she arrives in the small California Gold Rush town. Still, there's plenty of history as well as anticipated romance with her favorite cowboy, Jake Norris. But when the owner of the local café goes missing, Paige is determined to find out why. Will she uncover a dangerous secret in the town's old mining tunnels, or will curiosity land her in over her head?

The Sadie Kramer Flair Series

A Flair for Chardonnay

When flamboyant senior sleuth Sadie Kramer learns the owner of her favorite chocolate shop is in trouble, she heads for the California wine country with a tote-bagged Yorkie and a slew of questions. The fourth generation Tremiato Winery promises answers, but not before a dead body turns up at the vintners' scheduled Harvest Festival. As Sadie juggles truffles, tips, and turmoil, she'll need to sort the grapes from the wrath in order to find the identity of the killer.

A Flair for Drama

When a former schoolmate invites Sadie Kramer to a theatre production, she jumps at the excuse to visit the Monterey Bay area for a weekend. Plenty of action is expected on stage, but when the show's leading lady turns up dead, Sadie finds herself faced with more than one drama to follow. With both cast members and production crew as potential suspects, will Sadie and her sidekick Yorkie, Coco, be able to solve the case?

A Flair for Beignets

With fabulous music, exquisite cuisine, and rich culture, how could a week in New Orleans be anything less than fantastic for Sadie Kramer and her sidekick Yorkie, Coco? And it is... until a customer at a popular patisserie drops dead face-first in a raspberry-almond tart. A competitive bakery, a newly formed friendship, and even her hotel's luxurious accommodations offer possible suspects. As Sadie sorts through a gumbo of interconnected characters, will she discover who the killer is, or will the killer discover her first?

A Flair for Truffles

Sadie Kramer's friendly offer to deliver three boxes of gourmet Valentine's Day truffles for her neighbor's chocolate shop backfires when she arrives to find the intended recipient deceased. Even more intriguing is the fact that the elegant heart-shaped gifts were ordered by three different men. With the help of one detective and the hindrance of another, Sadie will search San Francisco for clues. But will she find out "whodunit" before the killer finds a way to stop her?

A Flair for Flip-Flops

When the body of a heartthrob celebrity washes up on the beach outside Sadie Kramer's luxury hotel suite, her fun in the sun soon turns into sleuthing with the stars. The resort's wine and appetizer gatherings, suspicious guest behavior, and casual strolls along the beach boardwalk may provide clues, but will they be enough to discover who the killer is, or will mystery and mayhem leave a Hollywood scandal unsolved?

A Flair for Goblins

When Sadie Kramer agrees to help decorate for San Francisco's high-society Halloween shindig, she expects to find whimsical ghosts, skeletons, and jack-o-lanterns when she shows up at the Wainwright Mansion—not a body. With two detectives, a paranormal investigator turned television star, and a cauldron full of family members cackling around her, Sadie and her sidekick Yorkie are determined to find out who the killer is. Will an old superstition help lead to the truth? Or will this simply become one more tale in the mansion's haunted history?

A Flair for Shamrocks

When flamboyant senior sleuth Sadie Kramer's car breaks down outside a small Oregon beach town, the repair lands her in unexpected lodging above an Irish pub for St. Patrick's Day. With pub games, green beer, and a potbellied pig named Paddy in the mix, it's bound to be a unique holiday. But not all is what it seems in Irishton, especially when the owner of the pub turns up dead. An assortment of local characters could be guilty, but only one is the killer. Sadie and her sidekick Yorkie will need the luck of the Irish to solve the mystery.

The Moonglow Christmas Series

Mistletoe at Moonglow

The small town of Timberton, Montana, hasn't been the same since resident chef and artist, Mist, arrived, bringing a unique new age flavor to the old western town. When guests check in for the holidays, they bring along worries, fears, and broken hearts, unaware that Mist has a way of working magic in people's lives. One thing is certain: no matter how cold winter's grip is on each guest, no one leaves Timberton without a warmer heart.

Silver Bells at Moonglow

Christmas brings an eclectic gathering of visitors and locals to the Timberton Hotel each year, guaranteeing an eventful season. Add in a hint of romance, and there's more than snow in the air around the small Montana town. When the last note of Christmas carols has faded away, the soft whisper of silver bells from the front door's wreath will usher guests and townsfolk back into the world with hope for the coming year.

Gingerbread at Moonglow

The Timberton Hotel boasts an ambiance of near-magical proportions during the Christmas season. As the aromas of ginger, cinnamon, nutmeg, and molasses mix with heartfelt camaraderie and sweet romance, holiday guests share reflections on family, friendship, and life. Will decorating the outside of a gingerbread house prove easier than deciding what goes inside?

Nutcracker Sweets at Moonglow

When a nearby theater burns down just before Christmas, cast members of *The Nutcracker* arrive at the Timberton Hotel with only a sliver of holiday joy. Camaraderie, compassion, and shared inspiration combine to help at least one hidden dream come true. As with every Christmas season, this year's guests will face the New Year with a renewed sense of hope.

Snowfall at Moonglow

As holiday guests arrive at the Timberton Hotel with hopes of a white Christmas, unseasonably warm weather hints at a less-than-wintery wonderland. But whether the snow falls or not, one thing is certain: with resident artist and chef, Mist, around, there's bound to be a little magic. No one ever leaves Timberton without renewed hope for the future.

Yuletide at Moonglow

When a Yuletide festival promises jovial crowds, resident artist and chef, Mist, knows she'll have her hands full. Between the legendary Christmas Eve dinner at the Timberton Hotel and this season's festival events, the unique magic of Christmas in this small Montana town offers joy, peace, and community to guests and townsfolk alike. As always, no one will return home without a renewed sense of hope for the future.

Starlight at Moonglow

As the Christmas holiday approaches, a blizzard threatens the peaceful ambiance that the Timberton Hotel usually offers its guests. Even resident artist and chef, Mist, known to work near miracles, has no control over the howling winds and heavy snowfall. But there's always a bit of magic in this small Montana town, and this year's storm may just find it's no match for heartfelt camaraderie, joyful inspiration, and sweet romance.

Joy at Moonglow

Each holiday season is unique in the small Montana town of Timberton. New and returning guests bring their dreams, cares, and worries, and always leave with lighter hearts and renewed hope for the future. But no season has ever been as special as this one. Because, to everyone's delight, wedding bells will be ringing. Thanks to the heartfelt efforts of many and no shortage of sweet romance, this year will be the most joyful of all.

Evergreen Wishes at Moonglow

Christmas in the small town of Timberton, Montana, is always filled with holiday traditions, exquisite cuisine, and heartfelt camaraderie. When a majestic evergreen tree is placed in the center of town, inviting ornaments containing wishes, townsfolk and visitors are soon pondering what their hopes and dreams might be. Although wishes can't always come true, some just might with a bit of holiday magic.

Angels at Moonglow

The small Montana town of Timberton always provides a joyful Christmas retreat for visitors as well as those who live in the area. This year, an angel ornament project offers guests and local townsfolk a chance to reflect on others in their lives. As always, time spent together, exquisite food, and camaraderie allow guests a chance to trade worries for a sense of peace and hope for the future.

Additional titles:

Cranberry Bluff

Molly Elliott's quiet life is disrupted when routine errands land her in the middle of a bank robbery. Accused and cleared of the crime, she flees both media attention and mysterious, threatening notes to run a bed-and-breakfast on the Northern California coast. Her new beginning is peaceful until five guests show up at the inn, each with a hidden agenda. As true motives become apparent, will Molly's past come back to haunt her, or will she finally be able to leave it behind?

Sweet Treats: Recipes from the Moonglow Christmas Series

Delicious recipes, including Glazed Cinnamon Nuts, Cherry Pecan Holiday Cookies, Chocolate Peppermint Bark, Cranberry Drop Cookies, White Christmas Fudge, Molasses Sugar Cookies, Lemon Crinkles, Spiced Apple Cookies, Swedish Coconut Cookies, Double-Chocolate Walnut Brownies, Blueberry Oatmeal Cookies, Cocoa Kisses, Angel Crisp Cookies, Gingerbread Eggnog Trifle, Dutch Sour Cream Cookies, and more!

More Sweet Treats: Recipes from the Moonglow Christmas Series

Chocolate Crinkle Cookies, Amish Sugar Cookies, Yuletide Coconut Cherry Cookies, Almond Crunch Bars, Chai Tea Shortbread Cookies, Peanut Butter Chocolate Fudge, Peppermint Snowball Cookies, Cranberry Walnut Pinwheels, Gingerbread Kiss Cookies, Eggnog Cookies with Rum Butter Icing, Glazed Fruitcake Cookies, Dutch Letter Almond Bars, Crème Brûlée Cookies, Caramel Apple Cookies, Date Nut Torte Squares, Salted Peanut Cookies, Chocolate Waffle Cookies, and more!

For more information on Deborah Garner's books:

Website:
http://deborahgarner.com

Mailing list:
http://eepurl.com/bj-clD

❄

facebook.com/deborahgarnerauthor
x.com/PaigeandJake